An Asset to Wales

Berta Ruck
An Asset to Wales

 HUTCHINSON OF LONDON

HUTCHINSON & CO (*Publishers*) LTD
178–202 Great Portland Street, London W1

London Melbourne Sydney
Auckland Bombay Toronto
Johannesburg New York

First published 1970

*This book has been set in Baskerville, printed in Great Britain
on Antique Wove paper by Anchor Press, and
bound by Wm. Brendon, both of Tiptree, Essex*

ISBN 0 09 101960 5

For my friend Aled Vaughan

Contents

Contents

Acknowledgements

My grateful thanks are due to Mrs. Bambridge, Mr. Kipling's daughter, for permission to quote from her father's work; and to Mrs. Helen Rees for permission to quote from the works of her husband, John Llewellyn Rhys.

Chapter One
Prince of the Castle

I

'I cannot go on without the woman I love.'

Gentle, sad, but unmistakably resolute the words came clearly over the radio.

In my unlighted room I stood as if in the presence of the speaker, as did listening millions of others in this country and in others all over the world. For this was the voice of a King speaking to his Empire.

That night we heard the goodbye to us of Edward VIII. It ended, still resolute but cheerful—'and now we all have a new King—'

Next morning we woke in the reign of George VI.

Recorded parting words of the ex-monarch could only have come from one with in his veins the drop of Tudor blood. It brought in the Welsh sense of drama.

'God bless you, sir,' he said, bowing over the hand of the brother whom he had made a king. 'May you be happier than your predecessor.'

II

Please, may I now try to show you things as they were more than twenty years before that night of the broadcast?

Back, then, to that crowded day of glorious life, of tumult and shouting and spectacular show—June 14, 1911. Date of the first Investiture of a Prince of Wales to take place actually *in* Wales.

I had the luck to be there.

That summer my husband and I were on a visit to my parents. My father was Chief Constable of Caernarvonshire, and they lived then in a house called Bryn Teg, across 'the Aber' (its swing-bridge, now demolished, was still in full swing) and standing back a short run from the foreshore of the Menai Straits.

Caernarvon itself was—and is—a mixture of untouched beauty and of the starkest ugliness. Slate-roofed houses had cracked slate steps up to doors from which the cocoa-coloured paint had blistered and peeled. Doesn't the Castle make up for all? Magnificently constructed walls are drawn around the town and the quay like the arms of a stately mother who protects an ill-favoured child.

Strange that this fortress, like that of Harlech and others around the coast, was built by Edward the first in A.D. 1301 to keep the rebellious, insurgent mountain-Welsh from overrunning the civilised inland districts.

On this day of 1911, 'mountain-Welsh' were here to besiege the place in force; but it was to welcome a Prince with Welsh blood in his veins.

A General Holiday had been proclaimed for places of business all over Wales.

Most of her towns staged memorable Treats for her children. There were processions for them. Sports for them. Distributions of 'souvenir' prizes. Harlech, Conway, Criccieth, all the medieval Castles hung out their banners to the children's admiration. Church bells rang. Bands played in Parks. Along the gaily be-flagged street of Wrexham 500 children paraded. Surely many of them are still alive to remember this and the culminating TEA?

Otherwise, curiously, towns had been reported : 'very quiet'.

Portmadoc? Decorated but deserted. From Pwllheli one-fourth of the population had *disappeared* into the early morn-ning mist. *Gone?*

Naturally to Caernarvon.

Choruses of excited voices nearing railway-stations, special trains, coaches: 'Yes, yes! going to the Investiture, of course. . . . Taking Baby? . . . Never see anything like . . . Toot! . . . he's not all that little! . . . Not in our life-time whatever Investiture too he'll be good yes, indeed mustn't miss Pram sandwiches this chance no, no—'

How differently hundreds of these Welsh pilgrims would have reacted if a feature of their daily lives had been—as it was not, then—invented! Numbers might have decided to stay quietly at home and watch it in comfort on the T.V. 'See the whole excitement . . . better that way, too . . . From the start. See the Prince at Holyhead. With the King's Harbour-Master and the Lord Lieutenant of Anglesey! Getting off the Royal yacht . . . Train taking him across the Menai Bridge . . . Meeting his Escort at Griffith's Crossing—that minute Halt was still extant—see a "close-up" of the Prince in his grand State carriage on his way to the Goings-on.'

There was no television.

Along what would be the Prince's route early birds perched on roofs and walls before he could have set foot on Holyhead's decorated jetty.

Caernarvon's narrow old-fashioned streets had become a vast conveyor-belt of people, moving, moving, ever moving towards Castle Square.

On fair-days of our childhood a mass of mud and cattle driven down from hill-farms, today it was the flag-fluttering coveted vantage point for conveyor-beltfuls of people from North and South. People who'd been ready to rise in the misty dawn, travel in crowded discomfort; and prepared to stand for all the hours of a glaring June morning, as long as they got a *sight*—!

It was scheduled for midday. The town was filled up by eight.

'I say! You hurry! Or you'll never get through the blessed mob to your seats,' warned father.

We'd come up from our swim and met him on the drive from Bryn Teg, looking pessimistic in unfamiliar dark uniform and cocked hat, of all things on earth. Crowded public occasions—cum-official-responsibilities he always took with the tensest conscientiousness, though he couldn't have enjoyed them less. He was probably still jarred by an incident of the evening before.

He had come home wrathfully shaking a newspaper, one of those 'subversive Welsh red rags' (probably long-defunct) which roused all the Conservative Englishmen in his two-sided come-from. One of 'his' Policemen had brought it in to him.

'Look at this!' It might have been news of a bomb outrage. 'By *Jove*!' The only oath he ever uttered. 'Disgraceful thing ...'

'What is it, Arthur?'

'Disgraceful . . . fellows ought to be locked up . . . Richly deserve . . . Wouldn't have dared to print it in English!'

'What's it *about*?' asked Mother with a little tap of her foot. 'I can't read Welsh'—which she, *née* d'Arcy, was inclined to regard as a dialect of savage tribes.

Father took back the paper, cleared his throat, and indignantly translated

'There is much hanes (talk) here at present of some Prince of Wales who is coming to visit us. The truth is we have no Prince of Wales! The last Prince of Wales was Llewelyn ap Iorworth, treacherously murdered by the English in twelve-hundred and forty ...'

'*Printing* disloyal rubbish! Now!'

'But if this fair-haired English lad—boy—youth—who is coming amongst us were to knock at any cottage-door and

ask for a drink of water, we should give it to him, and
welcome!'

'Oh, Arthur, I don't call that very disloyal. They *like* his
coming!'

At all events many thousands of them outside the Castle walls
were waiting to welcome him in weather increasingly brilliant
and broiling. Boys who took to the water were lucky: they
swam about, cool, beside the quay-wall under the Eagle
Tower. Envied by Boy Scouts assembled at that point to
receive a word from Chief Scout Sir Robert Baden-Powell.
    Notabilities threaded their way through crowds not over-
quick to recognise strangers, but they discovered Mr. Asquith,
Mr. Baldwin. Mr. Keir Hardie was down on the programme
to appear among the Welsh M.P.s; he was looked for in vain.
However, the Member for his own Constituency was instantly
and rapturously greeted. In other words, Mr. Lloyd George,
debonair in Privy Councillor's garb, received his usual ova-
tion. Today he held further office. Entering, elaborately-
feathered cocked hat under arm, he strolled in under the eyes
of the waiting throngs—fewer than those outside, but still ten
thousand of them!—with his air, almost, of being King of the
Castle rather than the Constable thereof—a position held at
present by Lord Snowdon.
    Sitting in a labyrinth of rows of waiting spectators, I recall
seeing the high-set canopied dais, at the top of the slope under
the stone lions of a Tower, prepared for Royalty. What other
Royalty might it have been, IF that handsome young Welshman from Anglesey hadn't done so well in the French War
and come up to the English Court and won the heart of a
King's widow, the lovely Katherine de Valois? If they hadn't
become passionate lovers, married, perfectly respectably, but
secretly? If the secret romance hadn't also secretly resulted in
three baby boys—Tudors. If these hadn't been discovered,
proclaimed legitimate (which they in fact were!) taken from
their Mother and given an Earldom each . . . If, during fan-

tastic fighting over England, there hadn't been a Battle of
Bosworth and—'Ha! what's this?'

It was the entrance of the white-robed Arch-Druid of
Wales, leading in his procession of Bards, also robed, making
as they walked an alternate pattern of white, blue, white.

My husband had been surprised that Druids and Bards,
when robed for an Eisteddfod, 'did not look as if they were in
fancy-dress, but always completely natural'.

'Why shouldn't they look natural, Georgie? It's their working clothes!'

. . . That vast massed Choir! The continuous Concert had
been joyfully arranged to while away the long wait. 'Plaintive
exquisite sweetness of Welsh voices raised in old Welsh melo-
dies' was remarked by the Press. 'The rich-voiced choir singing so perfectly together that, in spite of the excitement they
gave to well-known lines, you could hear every word they
sang . . .'

Restlessness was growing around us . . . Scanning of wrist-
watches. Murmurs: *What's the time? . . . How far is the drive
from Griffith's Crossing? . . . Not more than three or four
miles . . . The time now?* Another flash of sun on wrist-watch.
Coming up to . . .

Sudden, shattering thrill! A simultaneous outburst of
noises startled the assembly into a still-set jig-saw of colour.

Dazzlingly clear against the deep blue sky above the Tower,
those trumpeters had raised their blazoned trumpets to their
lips and sounded loud welcoming blasts—Joined in unison by
the deep *Boom! Boom! Boom!* from great guns in the Camp.
And up—subdued by massive walls so that the sound reached
those in the Castle as no more than the shrill cry of a swift
that had been circling the Chamberlain's Tower—up from
Castle Square rose cheers and more cheers of greeting to—
The Prince!

III

Arrival of the State-carriage—We *heard* about that! Reception by Mayor and Corporation. Address of 'Welcome with all

the ardour and the enthusiasm which is characteristic of our nation'—It certainly is.

Leaning forward in the carriage the Prince read his reply, making reference to the 'historic town', to having already heard some of 'the famous singing' of the Welsh 'coming as it did from the heart as well as the head. . . . You bid me *Croeso* (welcome) so I will say'—followed words in Welsh. . . . We could lay bets that another David had helped with the rehearsal of 'Diolch o waelod fy nghalon i hen Wlad fy nghadau.'

After this successful effort the Royal lad jumped out of the carriage, running up the stone steps that bridge the moat. He stopped at the Castle doorway. Turned. Acknowledged the cheers with a simple naval salute, then entered the narrow doorway, followed by the two tall figures of his escort.

This was our first glimpse of that slight, boy's figure in its midshipman's rig.

So young! He didn't look as much as seventeen. . . .

He crossed to the Chamberlain's Tower which was guarded by a huge policeman.

The Prince beat sturdily upon the closed door. That was the drill. The door was opened to him, not by the Constable of the Castle. Apparently that was also the drill. He was received by debonair David Lloyd George *inside* the Tower.

Now for a break.

In the small, massive-walled dressing chamber the sun could stare in only through the long arrow-slit upon the glittering panoply as for Princes long-dead, into which he must change out of his plain Navy blue.

Three-quarters of an hour later—on the dot—entrance of King George V, resplendent in full Admiral's uniform side by side with Queen Mary.

Slender in those days. A half-unfolded Arum-lily with a soufflé on the top—That was how I saw her white sheath gown and high, light, fluttering hat. Behind her Royal parents Princess Mary (the Princess Royal) was also in white, of early girlhood flowering, and with a smaller soufflé on her not-yet-'up' blonde hair. Warmly acclaimed, they took their seats under the canopy and the stone lions. Eyes upon them were satisfied. Here was Royalty as it should be; and as it was on that day, required to be. Gracious. Aloof. Apart.

The Prince was summoned.

Out of that cool dim pool of shade he emerged into (Press caption) A FURNACE OF LIGHT AND COLOUR.

It must have hit him like a cosh.

Stiff upper lip kept was the drill. No hint of awkwardness displayed over the array of great ermine collared purple cloak, white tunic and hose. Dignity preserved.

With resolute dignity he moved between the commanding figures of his escort. Up to the steps, up the many steps, and into the gorgeous circle. I am glad I had not then read—it was not yet written!—*Family Album,* which describes the importance given by George V to meticulous 'rightness' of demeanour, dress, hair-cut, every *nuance* of correct gesture to be observed without fail by his son on every occasion.

Yes, I'm glad I did not fully realise, at the time I was watching it, just what an endurance-test was being given to this boy. I've thought of it since I've had boys of my own.

The Prince was mindful of all. He knelt before the King. Bowed his uncovered golden head. It could be seen that he was pronouncing, unfalteringly, the Oath of Allegiance.

'I, Edward Prince of Wales, do become your liege man of life and limb, and of earthly worship and faith and truth I will bear unto you, to live and die, against all manner of folk.'

Simple words of an idiom outdated! The ritual was heart reaching. It appealed to the hearts of all manner of folk. Drama-conscious Welsh folk were not far from tears when the King raised his son to his feet, kissed him on either cheek, placed the golden circlet (Crown of the old Kings of Wales) on that fair head, referred to him as *our most dear son Edward Albert Christian George Andrew Patrick David,* and invested him with the further regalia—girding him with a sword, putting a gold ring on his finger, and taking the letters patent from the Home Secretary, placing them in the left hand of the

Prince. Again the cheers rose. The Prince 'fixed' his crown on
his head with obvious relief that this part of it was accom-
plished . . . and that the Royal parents had *smiled,* not only
as encouragement! *The King's Smile* was to be noted in all
the papers, and the glances exchanged between him and the
Queen . . . the satisfaction of 'Mother and Father, of man
and wife were in their look.' The note of domesticity was
struck again and again. To no nation could it have appealed
more strongly than to the family-life-loving, democratic-
minded Welsh. Sincerely, they hoped that this day was a
'foretaste of a long and glorious career among his own people.'
Unfeignedly, 'they would love that boy.'

There was more to come.

A special correspondent captioned it

PRESENTATION OF THE PRINCE TO HIS PEOPLE
A PAGE OUT OF GRIMM

and declared that it had possessed all of a romantic, fairy tale.

I saw the Prince and the King and the Queen come hand in
hand down the steps that lead from the Castle to the balcony outside Queen Eleanor's window

which should be Queen Eleanor's *Gate.* This was where
Edward I, who had promised the Welsh chiefs that they
should have a Prince born in Wales, who could speak neither
English nor French (second language of the Court) and then
displayed to them the Queen's new-born baby. A hair-splitting
trick—forgotten on this day.

We were the 'populace.' Grimm always has a populace. We
had waited, long and faithfully, tired with standing, hoarse
with cheering, but the faithful populace still.

. . . there was 'The Castle' with towers, battlements, arrow-
slits, a moat . . . After Grimm's own heart. Even a dragon
was not wanting. Round the woodwork of the Balcony dragons
were blazoned in every colour (not only Y Ddraig goch, the
Red Dragon of Wales that goes forward.)

The Prince thanked the people of Wales in a voice reported to be 'clear and confident.' This must have meant effort; no loud-speakers in those days. He thanked them for their cordial welcome, hoping that this might be the first of many visits to their beautiful country. Tactful references he made to many links with the Past. 'My Tudor descent, the great title I bear, as well as my name David all bind me to Wales . . . a happy day in the Principality, which has brought you a new friend. He is, it is true, a young friend . . . I am very young . . .'

'There he stood, the very young Prince,' noted the correspondent, 'with his golden crown on his head, one hand holding aside the folds of his purple and ermine cape, the other on the maw of one of the balcony's carven dragons, a great black arrow-tongued fellow rampant.' Ill-luck to mention *black* at this point? But what a marvellous shot it would have made for the not-yet-invented T.V.!

The correspondent reassures us

The men and women of Wales will love that boy, and if in these modern times (1911) a black dragon lurks anywhere in Wales, he will be no more alarming than the one on which the Prince rested his hand this day.

That day could have provided another good television shot —except that it would have been instantly killed in the cutting-room!—which Father reported to us at supper that night.

Father, cocked hat correctly under arm, was stationed with 'his' Policemen by the State carriage in which the Royal Party was about to drive away. He was near enough to see the young Princess Royal ever mindful of Buckingham Palace protocol draw back to let her brother the newly-invested Prince of Wales, precede her. Near enough was Father to take in that very human gesture of a boy who, after long, glaring, hot hours of behaving graciously, of ceremony, speechifying, meetings and presentations to and of hordes of unknowns, of strain heavier than any he'd experienced in his seventeen years of life, was at the end also of his tether.

He gave his sister a little push forward, muttering petulantly, 'Get in, you little Ass!'

> *The tumult and the shouting dies,*
> *The Captains and the Kings depart.*

Late evening. The Aber ferry is at high tide. Black satiny waters; silvery reflections looping, glittering, quivering. Against that full moon rise silhouetted tall turrets of the old Castle; silent now.

(*Goodnight, sweet Prince.*)

Chapter Two
Postscripts to Pageantry

I

That Day of Pageantry and Protocol was followed by the Night of the Firework displays and Bonfires all over the Principality. Huge bonfires were set blazing to the skies above the heights of Moel-y-gest and of Snowdon.

Gradually as those flames died down, the old town of Caernarvon settled back like a tired dowager into ordinary life—plus a new talking-point. Hanes (gossip) about the Investiture.

For Aberystwyth, University town of *our College by the sea,* a great Day was made by—you've guessed it—The Navy.

At daybreak ships arriving from Holyhead were sighted on the horizon. As the sun rose they were enveloped, dramatically! in a heat haze. Can't you picture those huge shadowy Shapes looming through the mist? I see them half-real, resembling the vision of the stately Elizabeth galleon *The Mary of the Tower* as she appeared to the officer of the watch on the destroyer *Sea-pink* in my favourite ghost story, *Phantas.* Slowly, they moved towards their moorings at Castle Point, eagerly awaited by sightseers along the whole length of the Promenade, and gradually materialising from apparitions into

the Second Division of the Home Fleet under the command
of Vice-Admiral Sir G. Callaghan. He, we were told, had
arranged to receive the Mayor and Corporation in the morning and the Town Council would entertain 500 men of the
Fleet to luncheon in the Pier Pavilion. Invitations, too, had
been sent to the officers by the North Cardiganshire Tennis
Club for a garden party.

In the afternoon the ships—which were the *King Edward
VII* (the flag-ship of the Admiral), the *Agamemnon, Britan-
nia, Dominion, Hibernia* (the flag-ship of Rear-Admiral
George E. Patey), *Hindustan, Lord Nelson, New Zealand* and
Bristol—were thrown open for Inspection.

You can imagine the rush. . . . Girls and boys who had
never before seen a battleship could on this day of days be
marshalled by the man-o-wars' petty officers to walk on upper
decks thereof. Could gaze down from the Bridge. Adventurous old ladies could get 'almost as far as' the Turret. It was
one of this last who, looking up the range-finder, remarked
approvingly 'Ah, very handy when they're short of water!'

Shore leave had been granted that afternoon to hundreds of
men of the Fleet. Meanwhile their officers, such as had not
attended the garden party, were engaged in a cricket match
on the Vicarage field.

It is a safe bet that the traditional Good Time was had by
all. Including the local boatmen. They must have made a
packet.

One only hopes that in a ship not among these, a simple
young midshipman was relaxing among shipmates who could
be trusted not to rag him about his big role in all the pomp
of yesterday.

After those long sunbaked, gruelling hours of pageantry, of
dutifully looking, doing and saying The Right Things—some
of the last in Welsh of which he must carefully memorise the
correct pronunciation!—surely the Prince of Wales deserved
a rest?

II

Small rest was his during the years shortly to come!

1914 brought the First World War. In 1919, at a party in New York, I heard this report on H.R.H., given by Prince Murat, married to an American wife. He had an *Angst*-complex, I thought, about revolutions. He said to me: 'Only one thing saved the Monarchy for Great Britain during the War. Yours might have gone the way of all the others, I think, but for the heir to the throne, the Prince of Wales. That boy, that young boy, by his bravery in the trenches, and his charm of personality, kept it. The most Bolshie-minded private soldier would go anywhere and do anything for your Prince of Wales.'

The Prince had difficult enough things to do himself. And himself to go everywhere. All over (what were then) the Dominions he was sent on goodwill tours. He was the *Ambassador from Britain's Throne and type of all her race*—and, with his personality, his boyish, golden good looks, *plus* his position—was he a success! America affixed to him the label *Prince Charming*. Everywhere the Prince went he was mobbed by enthusiastic fans. They nearly tore him to pieces.

After an early youth of too-hard restrictions and toeing the line of the Done Thing, this indiscriminate popularity had its effect. Inevitably the pendulum swung. He was over-confident that he would always be able to do whatever he wished, even before he came to the Throne.

III

The reign of Edward VIII—lasting months only!—was to be a kaleidoscope of Romance, of gathering storm-clouds, and hectic gaieties.

Clouds over the splendour had been gathering faster. Blackening. A King, still young, ardently in love, faced those in power who now could love only the ancient regime. There was a time of conflicting 'statements', of rumours, denials. Iron

Tradition encountered resolution as obstinate. How long that time seemed to a nation waiting in suspense! Not since the time of Richard the second, more than five centuries back, had a King of England announced his Abdication.

It was shattering for several reasons. One was the quick *volte face* in many quarters. The revelation that, except for a handful of 'trusties', a favourite has no friends.

He had said: 'I am prepared to go.' A page of history turned. He went.

I had the chance to set eyes on him again once, in 1938.

IV

'Only over the dead body of that man will the Duke of Windsor be assassinated.'

These words were muttered to me in the hall of the Hotel X in Vienna. I was there with an American journalist-friend who had invited me to come with him to see 'the Windsors', whose doings he was covering, set out for their week-end which they were to spend in the country home of the Rothschilds.

There we sat, in the entrance hall, against the wall with the announcements of plays and operas, facing the reception-desk.

Along came this huge, grim-jawed Scot, the Duke's bodyguard. Accurately, from the look of him, described by my escort. He passed out to the big black car waiting just outside the hotel entrance.

Next, a neat soubrettish little person carrying a small dog.

The Duchess's maid.

She passed on, out.

'They'll be down in a minute. Don't seem to look at them, will you?'

'Of *course* not!'

Without looking—which is a fact most women learn without difficulty—I saw them come quickly down. He was in a dinner-jacket without a coat. Deeply sun-tanned in contrast to his glinting fair hair, he looked less than his age. He always has. He still does, I expect. The Duchess was, as ever described in the Press, the epitome of elegance. Slim, in a black frock so simple that it must have been cut by a master. Her dark hair, slightly waved, was centre-parted in the mode of that month in that year of the 'Thirties, and drawn down on each side of her composed oval face, which was (apparently) un-made up, the accent being on the blue of her eyes.

Even if I hadn't known the story, hadn't heard that here was an ex-King with the wife for whom he had given up a throne, popularity, even the love of all but a handful of faithful friends, I think I should have sensed that there was *something* about them that hedged them. Arrestingly. Movingly, in their quiet, take-it-for granted dignity. It was unforgettable. The Duke gave up his key at the desk and followed her out.

The big black car started. They were gone, driving through Vienna's animated evening streets towards the mountains of Austria—which have always seemed to me like taller sisters of the mountains of Wales.

Chapter Three
'For Those in Peril'

I

'Well O! . . . Didn't you hear it blow in the night? Terrible gale! All night it—'

Boom! through the wind that was loud on the doors and windows of John Bell's house by the sea.

Excitement at kitchen breakfast! I'd dropped my porridge-spoon.

'What was that noise, Mamaly?'

Reply lost in the clumping of sea-boots as John Bell jumped to it.

'Distress-signal from some ship.' Had he said it or was it told to me next day?

Bang! Bang! Loud! Near! Two rockets fired from the Pier were to call out the Aberdovey Lifeboat.

John Bell, massive in oilskins, was already off. Out. Gone! After him pelted young Edda Bell—*Not* Dickie and Sally, they couldn't have been born? Flash-backs do at times get superimposed. I know that on other occasions the whole family would have been hot-footing it on his heels. 'Baby-Brother' (mine) was not yet on this earth. That I do know. I was still an only child . . .

Cry from Mrs. Bell . . . 'Too cold for the little girl! . . . You stay with me, dear—'

What a hope. Mamaly Davies the little Welsh nursemaid had tugged my small thick coat off the peg in the hall. Got me buttoned inside it. Pulled my red woolly Tam on down to my eyes.

'Quick, now, darling—' Clutching me by the hand she bore me along with her up the gale-swept street. . . . Half the village is out for this (Who'd miss it?) I get the flash-back of one wild rush—Clouds scud across the sky. Gulls scream and soar. High tide splashes over the chains that loop from post to black-topped white post of the Prom. Driven along by the wind we scurry towards the big Lifeboat house . . . (which now is Mr. Gray-Jones's workshop.)

Clear in my mind's eye is the picture of those twelve Lifeboat men—oilskinned giants! Strong as cart-horses, six to a side, they haul the great boat—(No motor-engines in those days!)—out, and down the wet slipway where I play when it is fine. . . .

Shouted orders in Welsh. . . . Twelve other giants—'John Bell with them, look, cariad!'—clamber swiftly aboard, are pushed off, and bend to the oars. I know it is called that! Mamaly had sung me that hymn, *Pull for the shore, sailor, pull for the shore! Heed not the raging waves but bend to the oar!* . . . Water looks dirty as the water in our bedroom basin when I'd had a good wash after playing with the sanded seaweedy pebbles, 'my stone dollies' . . . Waves lift the lifeboat . . . High, high! *Down* . . . Up again, high!

We scurry back along the road we came . . . Heads to the wind, spray in our faces; we don't see the boat now, but we run as if to race the lift and fall of those oars. They are far ahead . . . We are on the sands now . . . all crowding together . . . staring towards the white horses on the Bay beyond the Bar. . . . Voices chattering over my head . . . 'My husband says it's a hool gale . . . something awful, all night! . . . Well indeed it's a wonder she's still afloat. There she is, look!'

I was too small.

Someone made room, pushed me in front.

'That's it, Love . . . See?'

'I see it! I see it!'

I see it now, as I write. The ship small and black against
the dark-grey distance. Tossing, tossing like a toy thrown
between flying clouds and leaping sea. The mast, aslant . . .
Rigging like a loosened skein of knitting. In it, look! a man's
shape, clinging to the mast . . . waving, violently waving an
arm . . . I can't see the boat . . . sea hides it . . . only the man,
waving from the ship. . . .

Voices of crowding villagers. . . . 'Waving to them in the
boat . . . to make haste . . . oh, Duw! *Hurry,* hurry . . . ! hurry
quick they'll all be drowned else—'

'Will they all be drowned, Mamaly?' I appeal to a flapping
skirt. 'Mamaly, *will* they?'

Quick curtain. The whole scene vanishes. It's a way of these
memory flash-backs. Out! I just don't see what came next.

At bedtime (I think) I was told there'd be plenty *coed-bach*
(firewood) for us to pick up on the beach when the tide goes
down tomorrow. Driftwood she was, the *Mary Jane* out of
Liverpool . . . 'Smashed to pieces by the waves on some big
old sandbank on the Bar! Yes, yes, the crew was all saved . . .
Taken off every man! by our lifeboat, in the last minutes.
Captain last to go from the ship, and who d'you think was
mate, Mrs. Bell? Some Aberystwyth man, used to be very
friendly with— You know! young girl from here before she
married that—'

The wreck of the *Mary Jane* provided a gossip-point for
days.

II

The storm-motif surged back upon my consciousness when I
was of the age to read. That is, to devour with greed any
book that fell into my paws.

Father saw to it that I 'got' Dickens as they used to say a
child should get measles, early in life. Thanks to Father I 'got'
David Copperfield and David's mixed crew of friends. Before
I could spell their names I fell for the attractive Steerforth.
More thrilled than any Grown-up could be was I over the
historic storm, surely the most vivid ever written? Waves

'*monstrous as mountains*' thundered in, broke to pieces, rolled
back leaving deep undulating valleys (through which '*sometimes storm-birds skimmed*'). Storm, which to David seemed
a '*rending and upheaval of all Nature.*' Ham Peggotty (whom
I 'saw' exactly like our landlord-and-friend John Bell, sailor's-
cap at an angle over short, metal-strong curls, glint of gold
rings in his ears, fighting face, figure of heroic build as born
to rule the storm)—struggled out into the tempest with coiled
rope in a bid to save from the floundering vessel the man who
had stolen his girl—but both he and Steerforth perished in
that effort.

My sub-ten imagination took the pictured storm-drama
right away from Yarmouth and set it off the Bar and the
Estuary of Aberdovey.

III

Storms that rose more than a hundred years back are now the
theme—not of fiction but of a true bit of family history.

Letters, taken out of the cherished archives of our Nain,
concern one of her young Uncles. A forebear of our own, then,
on the Welsh side.

Here is the first :

I do hereby certify that Lieut. Richard Jones, R.N., served
as chief officer at the Coast Guard Station at Whitby under
my inspection from the 2nd day of July 1829 until the date
hereof, that he did, in the most courageous and intrepid
manner and at the imminent peril of his own life, and that
of his boat's crew, save the Crew of the Brig *Smails* of
Whitby on the 26th of January 1830, likewise the Sloops
William and *George,* and *Catherine* and *Ann* of the 29th
January 1830, for which humane and praiseworthy conduct
he has been awarded a Gold Medallion from the Committee of the National Institution for the preservation of
lives from shipwreck. And I further certify that he has per-
formed his duty in every respect to merit my warmest
approbation and esteem, and I have much pleasure in

recommending him as an excellent, zealous, indefatigable and determined Officer, and is well deserving of promotion.

Given under my hand at Whitby this 5th of July 1830

(Sgd) JAMES MORGAN

Inspg. Comr.

Never mind the Pre-Victorian pomposity of the Eighteenth Century style; disregard all but what it *means*; briefly, isn't it a 'chit' of which his kin today might feel rather proud?

The following year our Richard Jones broke his own record.

In January 1831 he, at the peril of his life and in swimming through the surf, did assist in saving the life of a man and of a boy off the wrecked sloop *Mary Anne* of Sunderland. The citation goes on :

Likewise on the 12th December last during a heavy gale of wind, the Sloop *Northfield* was wrecked, on the Whitby sands, he did in the most fearless manner at the imminent risk of his life, wade and swim through a heavy surf to the vessel, and procure help.

(Just like Dickens's heroic Ham Peggotty)

by which means the crew were saved. For such noble and praiseworthy exertions the Committee of the Royal National Institution for the preservation of life from shipwreck have awarded a gold Boat to be affixed to a Gold Medallion voted to him on a former occasion. And I beg most forcibly to add that his uniform conduct, his meritorious and active exertions have always been most conspicuous, and call forth my warmest approbation. I beg to recommend him to my Lords Commissioners of the Admiralty as an officer highly deserving of Promotion.

Given on the 28th January 1831

E.P.N.

'Your best agin that!' as the card-player shouted in *The*

Experiences of an Irish R.M. 'Throw down your jack!' (Ace?)

IV

Again and again in this day and age the Jack is thrown all along the shores that round our coast. Up to the present time the records come in of distress signals from ships answered at speed by 'the fearless and praiseworthy exertions' of the Royal Lifeboat Service.

At the end of World War One the papers had a brief notice of a rescue that had meant dicing with Death for all the lives concerned.

This had been off the coast of Yorkshire. . . . County that spells for me *1912, Speeton* . . . By the pilot's cottage, a sloping solid white bank of Mrs. Sinkin pinks smells 'like Eden ere the fall'. Precipitous path down to the sea with the baby carried in the sling across O.O's shoulder. . . . Rocky beach where we sat among the rusted boilers from some schooner long ago gone down.

That news-item of the 'Twenties got me to the point that I, once more on the Welsh coast, felt I *had* to write to the Life-boat's captain—to my shame the name has gone from me—sending congratulations to all and asking that the *small* cheque enclosed might be taken as a mark of great appreciation.

The Captain wrote back to thank Dear Madam and asked with native forthrightness if this money had been meant, special, for '*our* lads' or to go to the National Life-Boat funds?

I replied at once that this had been meant as a small tip for the lads.

V

A generation further on from the lads of the last-mentioned '*noble and praiseworthy exertions*' as these would have been termed in a citation of 1830—lads are still at it.

They will be called out, and will jump to it while gales still rage and men are still in peril on the sea.

—Remind me this year to send for Christmas cards issued to benefit the funds for the National Lifeboat Institution.

Chapter Four
Parents—and Pals

How many 'wild centuries' is it since you heard the phrase *'Our Elders and Betters'*?

Think back....

Did you ever *use* it, even as a crack? Or had it been dismissed already as an old-hat contradiction-in-terms? Yes? Ah, that gives your (circa) *date*. It also tells me what, in one thing at least, you are *like*.

You may not be Hippies, Trendy Types, or whatever they call them by the time this is in print. You may not necessarily bleach your nice dark hair (if feminine) or wear it shoulder-length (if male).

You are, however, on Christian-name-and-completely-equal-terms with your parents.

You probably share or freely discuss with them your likes or hates in faiths, films, friends, food and drinks, dieting, pop, and politics—as well as more controversial topics, which you would be shocked to hear *me*, at my age, mention. So I won't. I have taken to heart some young poet's comments on *'the shocking laughter of The Old.'*

To return to you Young and your Parents.

You pinch each other's new make-up or, if you're old enough to need it? your after-shave lotion. 'Respect' is a giggle-word, but, you and the parents, you're glad to say, Get Along.

So you and they are the civilised New Pals.

Well! We—my brothers, sisters and I, all eight born late-Victorians—were quite good friends with our Parents.

But we never called our Father and Mother, our Aunts, Uncles, or even our senior Cousins, by their unabridged Christian names.

We referred to them as The Grown-Ups.

Goodness knows there were plenty of them! Those were the days of recklessly big families! One cousin of my father's had fourteen sons and two daughters. There were 'only eight' of us. Not really so reckless. Not such a problem to feed, with prices at eightpence a pound for good Welsh mutton. Red-currants, for the jelly, were picked off the bush. 'Tattuss' were dug out of the garden. So were other vegetables. Bread was baked, jam was made at home. Flavours deep-freeze never knew simmered deliciously through Welsh kitchens. Innocent of handy packet soups, cake-mixes, and food-preservatives. The only things preserved were our digestions. These remained, in our late maturity, those of healthy animals.

We spent most of our childhood in the still-unravished depths of Merioneth—or Caernarvonshire.

All our lives we had been used to hear ourselves referred to as 'The Children'—long after we'd *left* childhood. After we'd left school. Were out in the world, in jobs. Trying to make our way in it. Acquiring new friends, other interests, values, other outlooks on life—In all of which our Grown-Ups had no part. For now we were *Away*. And *'Away'* seemed to some of us at least, at that time, so very much more interesting than 'There.' Behind park-palings of Victorianism. That was where our Grown-ups had been brought up. That was where they remained.

Or did they?

I told my Mother I had been to see Galsworthy's play; *The Silver Box*.

'You,' I said, 'would probably be shocked—'

I remember Mother's impatient little tap of the foot, her spontaneous flash of exasperation.

'Shocked? I am shocked at *nothing*. Only'—and here I was myself censoriously a little shocked at her protest—'I have to PRETEND to be, because of The Three Little Girls!'

Those three younger sisters were still taking it as a matter of course to be addressed, on Sundays, as Thou. (*My good child know this; that thou art not able of thyself etc.*)

It was only then I began to see Mother and her generation with new eyes, more understanding. There was a slight tinge in it of feeling *sorry* for the Grown-ups! I had even less tolerance for the 'Park palings' of Victorian ideas, though. And some impatience at our being considered, still! as the children.

'The children will be home for Christmas!'

Home now meant our Grown-ups' white house Esgair, set high above the road that leads to the Corris valley in Merioneth. Nain's Nain had lived there. It looked just as it had looked in our grandparents' time. *And* in their grandparents', to judge by the date on the two-tiered oaken wedding-chest, elaborately carved and bearing also the initials M. O. M. for Margaret and Oliver Morys. (Oliver and Morys were used as Christian names 'after' them, right down the family.)

'All the Esgair furniture is Genuine Antediluvian,' I declared in the *meant-to-shock* flippancy of the Then Young. 'Wedding-chests for Mrs. Ham, Mrs. Shem and Mrs. Japhet before they went Arking with the Noahs!'

Adolescents and young adults passed through that disdainful phase.

At least the Esgair furniture, carpets, curtains, feather-beds, portraits, its ante-room's walls darkened with sombre-framed prints of *Scenes in English History, Cromwell at his Daughter's Death-bed, Boadicea Haranguing Her Troops* (though surely she was Queen of the Ancient Britons, the Brythons, nothing to do with the English?)—Esgair's other pictures, too, the water-colour of Nain in a poke-bonnet with her little boys in

peaked caps and long belted blouses over trousers on the
beach at Aberdovey, the big steel engraving *Crossing the
Brook* and the others—all the objects had one feature in common. Strangely enough it became, presently, a reassuring, even
a welcomed feature, an asset. They were *Always There*.

As they'd Always *Been*.

Father and Mother, too, were just the same as they'd always
been. Father, big, gipsy-ishly dark and ruddy, deliberate of
movement, reserved. A man of few words, except when he
uttered—suddenly!—some dry shrewd comment on something we should never have thought he'd noticed.

Mother, in contrast, was fluent of speech and gesture, with
her gift of mimicry, her gush of girlish laughter. Brightly
interested in anything that was going on—'Sit down and tell
me *every detail*!' she would beg 'children' returning from a
visit or a party. Ready as the Athenians was Mother 'To tell
or to hear some new thing'. Pink-and-white complexioned,
blue-eyed under a mist of silver hair, she was openly vain—
why not? Avid for compliments! 'Your father,' she complained, 'never paid me a compliment in his life.' Father's only
reply, 'I paid you the biggest compliment I knew when I asked
you to marry me.'

Mother's retort, 'As if that COUNTED!'

'It's my day for writing to the overseas children today,'
Mother would announce—after two of us were in India (still
the British Raj) one—or was it another two?—in Canada.

We married. We brought along to Esgair, on visits, families
of our own. These were called, 'The Grandies'. Never 'The
Children'. We were that, to the end of her life. I am sure
she thought of us like that. Weekly she wrote to us—often by
some old nursery-name for each. There were times, I think,
when she was sad that she could not have *kept* us at that
stage. Perhaps other mothers have sensed that same fleeting
regret?

I made up one of my jingles on the subject, calling it:

SONS

When you were small, you two,
    I promised you
Ten bob the day I see you six foot tall.
    Ten years soon flew.
    Like rain on grass you grew.
Ten quid I'd give some days to see you small!

And this summing-up of the situation was launched at me by my elder son.

'You think we are Something Funny that's happened to *your babies*! Whereas your babies are Something Funny that used to be *Us*.'

When Mother left us, without warning, and in her sleep, one can only say it was as though gay music stopped, light went out, the glow of a hearth died down.

Alone at Esgair except for his devoted little maid Harriet, who is now Mrs. Lloyd and lives at the Lodge, Father said he would take on the weekly correspondence to the eight children, like Mother.

He did not possess, as Mother had, the pen of a ready writer. Or even any ordinary pen. Bamboos grew near a brook at Esgair. He cut for himself a nib at the end of a dried bamboo-stick. It was one of his several endearing little eccentricities.

How often I have seen him dip this primitive implement into the massive glass inkstand on the heavy writing-table in the old gun-room! I watch him pause; and sigh . . .

Knowing the labour this meant to him, we urged: *'Don't* bother about eight separate letters! Just write *"a round robin"*. For all of us. We'll send it on, from one to the other. Do that, Father.'

'*No.*' Father's mutter under the still-dark moustache was obstinate. 'I'll want to write about different things to all you

children, like Mother.' So every week each of his children,
whether living in the North of England, British Columbia,
London or India received a communication from Wales,
invariably signed (*'as if he wasn't any relation to us*!' we pro-
tested),

'*Yours Affly*

A. A. RUCK'

We are a long-lived family; he was in his ninety-second
year when he signed it for the last time.

At first it was hardly possible to take it in.

One of 'the children'—I am not now sure which—said
blankly : 'We have lost the last of our Grown-Ups'.

That brought it home to us what a link had snapped. As
well as our overwhelming personal loss; *Father,* of all people !

A whole generation had gone . . . Whether we had looked
upon these people with affection, resentment, ridicule, admiration, impatience as at an obstruction, refuge in some of our
own worries, deep down tenderness, all these things one after
another, or even at the same time, perhaps? we should always
sense the gap now that it didn't any longer matter how we'd
thought of them.

Knocked down was the barrier of defence that had stood
between us and looming, threatening *Change*; defence too
against *our* being 'The Old Ones', as long as these much older
ones were alive.

Now they *weren't*. . . .

As that brother—or was it a sister?—summed up : '*We* are
now the Grown-Ups.'

Chapter Five
Honours at the End

I

A Law unto himself—that, unquestionably, could be said of our eldest brother.

He had Father's habit of signing his correspondence by initials only. We even spoke of him as 'O.L.R.' He must have wished this done, I expect? He had a gift for impinging his own ways upon others—almost always getting away with it.

At the beginning of family-life I, his elder sister, was often jealously impatient. (*'Who does he think he is?'*) Later, I'd a theory. Probably true. He felt, quite genuinely, that he had the Right to Command. He was an Atavist.

Atavism, that throw-back to a vanished Past, to a simpler civilisation, can be a Force. The single-minded leader of brave uncomplicated men to whom his will was law!—was personified, often enough, in this man born in the late-Victorian era.

Perhaps the easiest way to 'give' him is to report his method of dealing with The Case of The Silver Cup stolen from the Mess.

This happened in India when we were still the British Raj. O.L.R. was serving in the 54th Sikhs, in the Punjab Frontier Force.

He told me of it in that low-pitched voice, half-growl, half-purr which has been described as The Ruck Mumble. I never

heard him raise it. The idea, I suppose, was LET THEM
LISTEN.

'There was this silver cup—'

Some Regimental trophy?

—'Missing. Must have been taken by someone. Got to be
found.'

The correct procedure, I imagine, would have been Guard-
room, interrogation of man after man who might have
handled the Cup at this time or that before its disappearance,
detention of the man or men who, it was hoped, might (as
put in the jargon of Police reports) 'help them with their
enquiries'—followed by Court-martial, conviction, sentence.

Not for O.L.R. the correct or 'done' thing.

In his own words: 'It must have been one of the men. So I
said, "Each man will now go out and fill a bucket full of sand.
They will pour out that sand on to the ground, until it makes
a big heap. In that heap the Cup will be found." It was found.'

As simple as that. Sounding like one of the perfect short
stories of the Old Testament.

'But,' I pointed out, 'the thief would not be punished for
the crime.'

'He was already punished,' said O.L.R. *'He knew I knew.'*

Some men are at their best and happiest when in full command of men. Preferably men of another race who regard him
as one of their own kin.

I was told by a friend of O.L.R.'s from those days 'Our
Head Native Officer of the Guides in early 1914, while our
Senior Officers were away serving "somewhere in France"
remarked that O.L.R. was an "Asal Pathan". This was the
highest compliment he could pay him. . . . *"Asal"* means
"real" or in his language "Pukka".'

Too early by far, as Father had mournfully said, O.L.R.
retired from the Indian Army, from among the people who
best understood him. He was not to be dissuaded. *'Better be
first'* (he thought, like the Longfellow character quoting
Caesar) *'in a little Iberian village Than be second in Rome . . .'*

Yet he brought back echoes of the Old Army when he
insisted that Father—who had ceased years ago to be a serving

soldier, ought, must, should have a funeral with military honours—a firing-party over the grave.

Since our brother next in age to himself lived in distant Canada, O.L.R. descended upon the youngest of our brothers. Also Indian Army (retired) this one also now lived in Wales. He read much in the Welsh language, out of which he later translated several books and some verse. This confirmed him in the immutable conviction that the Welsh people and their language are extraordinarily akin to the Persians, their speech and their temperament. (Mountain folk, in fact.)

Of him O.L.R. demanded if he had any khaki left?

'No. Only mess-kit. In any case, retired people who wear uniform without permission might get run in.'

'Oh, I don't care a damn about that,' said O.L.R. (well in character.) 'Father was a soldier for twenty years. Served in India. Afghan Campaign 1879. I am going to have Father given a proper soldier's funeral.'

After which he loped off. Yes, he had the noiseless loping movements of the big-game hunter. That too was a relic of antiquity when wild in woods the noble savage ran. He loped off to make his arrangements at Llanidloes.

He lived at that time near that market-town in his 'little Iberian village' the Van. High-set among mountains of which the view, he insisted, was exactly like the Himalayas. 'They're higher, of course. Sky-line's the same shape.'—Flashback of his shack, as he called the bungalow. It was reached (just reached) by car up a steep bumpy track, flanked on the right as you went up by a bank coloured by the gold of gorse, purple of heather, blue of scabious. 'Flowers the same as on the Foel,' he'd pointed out. Away far below to the left gleamed Bugeilyn, the Shepherd's Lake. Shearing of the small agile mountain sheep still takes place beside it, but it might well have been called The Lake of the Fishermen. Brothers, a brother-in-law, uncles, cousins, a nephew, of mine, have all spent absorbed days at Bugeilyn. Many's the delicious plump trout that's been bestowed on us at Aberdovey.

O.L.R. assembled the Llanidloes Territorials and—with or
without official right to do so?—gave them their orders . . .

This was towards the end of 1939's uneasy summer. Father
would have missed the start of World War II (we were often
to feel glad about that.) It was July. Least flowery of months.
Woods were thick under the monotonous cabbage-green
foliage which Father each year deprecated. The whole Corris
Valley had been unsmiling, that afternoon. . . . Tall, aloof
pines . . . small pointed arch . . . Gate into the downhill Church
path . . . Angular slate tomb-stones . . . It was all of a piece.
Grim! One touch of beauty—The cushion of massed deep-
purple violets tied with a ribbon in the colours of Father's Old
Regiment. Father's eldest nephew Dick Atkin, accompanied
by Dick's daughter Nancy, had searched London for that
ribbon and for the little silver horse, the Regimental crest.
Lovely of them to bring this, with the card 'for dear Uncle
Arthur . . .'
    In the little dim Church, the Choir had arranged to sing
the hymn which, next to the old Welsh tunes, was his favourite.
    'Lead, Kindly Light, amidst the encircling gloom.'
    Suddenly, it happened! Gloom ceased so hopelessly to
encircle us. . . . Why?—Down the steep side-road from the
Braich Goch Hotel to the Church, trundled those two big
motors and out trooped that posse of Caernarvonshire Police.
These could none of them been the original *'Father's* Policemen', as we as children in Caernarvon used to call them!
They were a generation too recent. . . . Aren't we warned that
it's a sign of approaching old age when all soldiers, all policemen we see begin to look *so young*? Boyish, these looked.
Younger than Father's *Number Nineteen,* in Caernarvon
days when he came for boxing-practice with our brother
Richard and had been heard to gasp laughingly *'No more,
Dick, by damn!'*
    That gay memory brought comfort, even though Number

Nineteen might now be of grandfather-age among this contingent? The present Chief Constable had rung up to ask if it would be liked for him to bring along some of the men as a mark of respect to the late Chief Constable? He had been assured that it would be liked. So, here they came. Touching? . . . It was lucky that two of us—only two, my youngest sister and I—could do the 'done thing' and keep the 'stiff upper lip', as we went up to say, steadily, 'Thank you. This is appreciated.'

Father, who had served twenty-six years in the Police Force— Worrying years many of them! Little as he had enjoyed the County Council Committee side of his duties!—had always got on perfectly with 'his' policemen. Had managed, too, that his men were also respected and liked. Even during the Tithe-riots when he had had to appear with them on duty during forced auctions at farms when scenes could have arisen. The owners' goods were sold, before their eyes, to pay for tithes to the Church which the Non-conformist farmers refused to acknowledge. Father had reported one occasion when, at the end (after an impassioned anti-tithe harangue by a fluent brown-haired young fire-brand of the name of David Lloyd-George, after the grandfather-clock, the oak-chests, the corner cupboard and other antiques had been knocked down to the highest bidders who would probably see to it that these possessions would get back to their home in time), after all this, a traditionally sumptuous farm-house tea, was 'sat down to' by the farmer, his wife, his friends and supporters, our Father, 'his' Policemen, and young Mr. Lloyd-George. That orator, putting an elbow on the long table had leaned across it to remark amicably: 'Isn't this *Celtic,* Colonel Ruck? Would this happen anywhere *but* in Wales?'

Long years afterwards, when he was the guest of honour at my Club in London the famous Welshman had said of Father, 'We all know that *he* always played the game'.

In Father's time, too, there had also occurred the more serious disturbances of the Penrhyn Quarry Strikes. Father, with 'his' Policemen, was liable to be summoned at any hour. He was once approached with the request to send for reinforcements of Police from neighbouring counties.

Here Father dug in. His Welsh blood spoke: 'I shall not require Police "from another County". I shall not require them even from another town.' (Meaning another town than Bangor, where 'incidents' were feared from indignant quarrymen and sympathising public.)

Authorities went behind the Chief Constable's back. Troops were summoned to deal with the situation. With what result?

Unpredictable as children, the population took the march-in of the red-coated soldiers (and I think there *must* have been a band) as a grand show, a pageant . . . 'something going on!' Grand to look at! Spectators stood, watching, applauding . . . (*'Wasn't it Celtic?'*) There had been no bringing in of 'strange old Police' from some other town. This would have been taken amiss. The veto on it was, one heard, counted to Father for righteousness.

And now it was fifty-three years since our Father had been a serving soldier, but still he was to have military honours at his funeral.

O.L.R. turned up—Not in khaki. We breathed again. That was in order, at all events. The detachment of Llanidloes Territorials, commanded by a Serjeant-Major, assembled. Smart in uniform. But—Complete with rifles? A firing-party? It would not, we understood, be a *feu-de-joie* (or *'furious joy'*, as it has been called by the troops). This was done by the men firing their rifles one after another on parade to celebrate various important anniversaries, such as Empire Day. Still . . . There were to be three volleys over the grave?

Some of us had an uneasy feeling that Father, ever reserved and anti-display, might not have approved. Would he even have barred having the casket (so small, for the ashes of so big a man) covered with the Union Jack?—'I think the little casket looked lovely!' Comment of his very young granddaughter Gwerfyl—Well, perhaps he would have minded that less? That flag had been Mother's property. It was 140 years old. During Father's years as Chief Constable it had draped the dining-room wall of the house we then lived in, under the framed notice for 'Grace and Favour' granted by George III to one of Mother's forebears.

It came to the end of the Service.

How bizarre are the tricks played upon us by Atavism with its anomalies, its powers for good or evil! It is assuredly *not* for good that War should still be allowed to exist? War, with its added hideous horror of bombs, and nuclear threats, should have been stamped OUT! Yet . . .

At the blare of military music, the tramp of marching feet, the clatter of cavalry accoutrements, at the flashing of sun on cuirass as the Horse Guards pass, the heart still lifts. . . .

So, as the shots rang out over the grave in little Corris Churchyard, followed by the bugler's sounding of the Last Post, the heart of an old soldier's most war-resenting daughter lifted and thrilled.

There was a touch of dry humour at the finish.

Dick Atkin, already a Law lord, said drily, 'It's all right as long as we keep out of the *Daily Mirror*.'

II

Bizarre, too, are the changes wrought (or uncovered?) by Time in the human character!

We were to see the high-handedness of O.L.R., whose will was law, give way to a basic gentleness. He had become as beloved in his Iberian village as he had been among the Pathans, Sikhs, Guides.

He, once the keen big-game hunter told me that now, at 80, he felt he was 'a murderer for having killed that tigress—'

Her beautiful striped skin had for long spread as a trophy over the ante-room wall at Esgair.

'—and for taking her from her cubs.'

Warmly affectionate, if sparsely-worded, was the interest he took, not only in his own 'cubs', in theirs, ('fine nippers' he said, proudly), in ours, and in those of the Ingrams of the

School House, the Van. Nothing would have shifted O.L.R. from his Welsh Iberian village. Yet, with his failing eyesight the bungalow was a danger-spot for him. The Ingram family took him in, complete with his Nell, the devoted black Labrador and his grey parrot, Sam, who contributed those piercing imitations of the first Bleep. Here O.L.R. remained to be cared for like a cherished relative for his closing years.

That September, with the young Rucks on holiday from Kent, two car-loads of us drove over from Merioneth for O.L.R.'s birthday picnic tea. September days in Wales can be baskingly warm.

This one wasn't.

Still, O.L.R. had settled on a spot bleakly higher up 'Where you got that view. Like the Himalayas.'

'Couldn't be much colder *there*?'

'Even in the snow—'

'Thanks be we've got the cars—'

The cars, with tea-baskets and provisions (here my nephew's life is ever tops) were parked on a flat bit of upland. Everybody gave a glance around the scene. Shivered. Laughed. Then made for cover.

There was sounded an old note of command.

'My sister Berta will sit out here (gesture) with me.'

Fortunately the ex-ice-breaking-winter bather (me!) knowing O.L.R. had the foresight to bring Aggie's big handwoven rug (it spread over both of us), an extra Thermos, and a King-sized breakfast cup and saucer of white and gold china which I had secured from Mr. Gale's antique-shop. (This was still the ornament of that Aberdovey side-street.)

The young, like ravens, brought provisions to us. Then, like ravens, flew back to shelter.

There we sat. On that flat bit of rock. Just above that precipice. Far, far below Bugeilyn glinted like steel. From the cars behind us a merry din of chat and giggling came in gusts on the piercing breeze. It is my last flashback of O.L.R. He didn't want to talk over the meal. He turned his direct blue gaze—the only one of Mother's eight children who had inherited Mother's eyes. So unfair! and then he lost one! He turned that arrow straight look, silently, across the gulfs of pure cold mountain air.

He looked at the Himalayan sky-line.

He looked down at the fishing-lake.

Finally he turned to me and uttered, 'Good cup of tea, that. Is this your rug?'

'A birthday-present for you, Oliver, if you'd like it? O.O.'s sister Agnes in Australia wove it on her loom.'

'Very good stuff. *Light* as well as warm. Oh. Thank you very much.'

Shortly after this we had all packed in again, said our good-byes at the school-house and were on the way home. The only cloud—Huddled in a corner of the car, one of the 'cubs' was near tears. He had so passionately wanted to stay on, to be allowed to fish in Bugeilyn.

'There'll be *plenty* of other times for you, later on!'

There wasn't to be another out-door birthday party for O.L.R.

We knew how he'd enjoyed every moment of this one.

For O.L.R., too, after he had left Earth's mountains and lakes, there were to be honours.

Thousands of miles away from Wales, an old friend of his hunting-days, Rajah Yusaf Ali of Mowara-Kahuta Rawalpindi in Western Pakistan, issued the command: 'At (such and such) an hour, as a mark of respect to Colonel Sahib O. L. Ruck, D.S.O., my whole village will keep the Two Minutes Silence.'

Chapter Six
Breadwinner

I

'This will interest you,' promised my friend Margaret who was driving me with her to Dolgellau where she was on a mission to the Red Cross. 'A father-to-son-for-generations business. Primitive, in a way.'

'What way?'

'Oh—People who are fussy about the newest hygienic methods might get a bit of a shock. But—Every time I'm near there I go in to buy a loaf at the Old Bakery.'

Our country is full of the Old This, the Old That.

Relics of some calling or craft that has changed its reason-for-being, keep the old name. The *Old Blacksmith's Forge* at Aberdovey, for instance. We, as small children peering in through an atmosphere of sparks flying upward, of a great heavily-sighing bellows, of the smell of hot iron on a horny hoof, watched fascinated! the way of Mr. Jones-Blacksmith with a horse.

What of it, now?—The Church Hall, home of W.I. meetings and of jumble sales for the British Legion, was built on the site.

An *Old Mill* is marked down for an Art Pottery.

An *Old Brewery* becomes the gadgetty home for a Bank Manager's retirement. The *Old Fire Station* is turned into the Secondhand Book-selling Establishment.

D

Two *Old Cottages* and a steep rocky bank on the road to Pennal have been transformed, by the forty-odd years' labour of my sister and her husband, into a veranda'd homestead in a garden so arrestingly colourful that summer visitors stop their cars to ask what *is* that? of the flowering Flame-tree, are invited in for a look-round, and find it well worth a contribution to the Fresh Air Fund.

A gifted architect in our village told his wife: 'I have found the place for us to live! Come and look at it.'

She went with him to look. It was *The Old Barn* tumbledown at that, with an old loft, over-shadowed by a big tree. She said: 'You're mad!' He wasn't. He just happened to be one of those people who see *Not the ploughed furrow, but the golden grain.*

He (and she!) have changed *The Old Barn* and its loft into the most unusual as well as the most habitable dwelling in the district. That big over-bearing tree gives just the right shade at the end of the wide terrace (ex-loft!) into which you step out of the big living-room with its enviable *wall*—built-in!—of books. The kitchen would be any Housewife's Choice.

Not every *Old Something* has thus come up in the world!

Once, when I had to give a 'talk' in the North of England, the hospitable lady who put me up for the night told me she also owned, just over the border from Scotland, a dilapidated house where Mary Queen of Scots stayed on the last occasion when she had gone hunting.

The place had gone down and down. Finally it came on the market. It found no bidders. Except for one firm. They saw possibilities of it run as—*a pig farm.*

'A Queen's Old Hunting-Lodge?' exclaimed its owner in horror. She was young, but definitely Old-Times-Romanticist. 'I'd rather let it die with dignity and crumble into the earth!'

II

We arrived at the Old Bakery. Unlike other survivals, it's alive on the old lines, continuing to remain quite simply the place where bread is baked.

It stands, this authentic chunk of Old Wales, in a back street of Dolgellau, that county-town of ins-and-outs, of ups-and-downs, all bafflingly inconvenient for motor-traffic! and it looks as if it could have held its ground there since the time of Cadwaladr and all his goats.

'Shakespeare,' I wrote, unnecessarily to my Bard-addict son, 'and don't tell me the Man didn't have at least a trickle of Welsh blood. How else could he have drawn Sir Hugh Evans with his "pribbles and prabbles"? Or his Captain Fluellen, spelling it that way so that English play-goers should know how more or less to pronounce his name? Or his Glendower with the chip on his shoulder—"I can talk English, Lord, as well as you".' But this chapter is about *The Old Bakery*.

Outside, solid as Cambrian Rock. Long, slate-roofed, grey-walled. Built of boulders hauled down, no doubt, from the mountainside by a working-party of sturdy short black-haired Iberians bossed by a Captain of the Roman Legion. Well, any-how! that was what it looked like from the street. Windows were too small to show any shop-name. A board was put up painted in clear block capital D. E. ROWLANDS, BAKERY and the picture of a square loaf (to ram it home.)

Inside, equipment was of (contrastingly) modern date. Middle—or even Late Victorian. Ponderously sizeable, meant to last. You got a general impression of brisk, con-scientious, expert and cheerfully-carried-out industry going on amongst a surround of disregarded clutter from four succes-sive reigns.

One end of this interior was taken up by the high-set baking-oven. Into its cavernous maw a baker in a white ephod and a linen tam-o'shanter was pushing a long-handled spade spread with blobs of dough.

A king-sized open crock of dough stood ready on the floor. A small woman wearing two large aprons stood by it at the long table which took up the middle of the place. She was fill-ing with dough the round scoops in a plateau—it reminded me of the trays an air-hostess brings round for lunch on the 'plane—to make smaller buns or rolls.

These, too, were pushed into the oven.

III

Interval. I was introduced by Margaret as a writer who would like to see the place, and to buy a loaf. The two workers-of-the-world looked at me as at someone they hadn't seen before and of whom they were wondering from where she came? When Margaret added that I sometimes spoke on the B.B.C., the sun came out. They shook my hands. The white-ephod-girt baker (he was not Mr. Rowlands the boss who came in anon) fished a chair-cushion—or would it be a square of canvas folded into four? out of clutter at the back. Covering it with wrinkled brown paper he set it on a bench, telling me with a smile, 'You see? You get V.I.P. treatment here.'

Remembering what Kenneth Harris had told me about the prestige that used to hang about *a name seen in print* having been lost to the prestige of a *name heard on the wireless,* and feeling partly abashed and partly thankful that this was true, I sat down, to glean information.

This evidently had to be a mutual affair. Miss Mary Harris of the two aprons, having volunteered her name, that she had worked here for thirty-five years and that she was all Welsh, 'But *not* one of these Nationalists who wanted everything separate—What was the use? Keep friends with the English, I think, they're our next-door neighbours, aren't they? You have to be friendly with neighbours, it's not as if they lived right away from us, is it? There's no sea between us, it's *not like the Irish*! Pity you didn't come here on Friday, it's our day to make fruit-cake, no fruit cake today, I'm sorry!'

She told me where she was from and paused enquiringly, but I left India out of it for the moment. I wanted to hear more about her. She seemed pleased to hear that from where I came today was recognisably near, and that my people were 'from' not far from Machynlleth. She seemed slightly surprised that I had lived in other places . . . but now her buns were ready.

How good they smelt!

She gave me one all breathing-hot, to see what it was like (delicious!)

I thanked her in Welsh.

'Oh! you speak Welsh!' she said approvingly in the vernacular.

'*Very* little,' I apologised, also in the vernacular. (At least my accent will pass.)

'You *speak* it same as I do. *Pronounce* it all right, I mean,' she continued in English, whether out of politeness or because more could be said I don't know.

The business didn't deliver much, I understood. Didn't have to. People *came*. Knew the *hours*. Pity, she said again, that I hadn't come on a Friday; fruit-cake, made in long pieces, cut off by the pound, five shillings a pound, some people came for it every week.

A number of 'regulars' arrived as I sat. Loaves were pushed into plain white bags and carried off in shopping-baskets. The place was evidently 'doing' as it deserved.

Mr. Rowlands came in, a tall man with an air of authority. (I heard afterwards that he was very musical, the Conductor of the Dolgellau Male Voice Choir.) He sent a quick appraising glance round the premises, nodded, came over to me—I had an impression that *somehow* he had already ascertained what I did and from where I was, shook hands kindly but silently, and went out.

The big black oven-door opened and shut smoothly as poured cream! on its iron and brass fittings. I got up to read the embossed lettering on the panel above it—

FRED HUNT LTD.
HILTON. WALES
1885

'Two years before Queen Victoria's Jubilee,' I said. 'One of the few dates I remember. We had mugs with her picture. A crown on her lace cap and veil, and the broad blue ribbon of the Garter curving over her breast.'

Also I remember that summer of 1887 because it never rained for the whole of that magic holiday which we—only four children then, and one baby—the first Welsh-born baby of our family—spent on Llandwyn Island, at the furthest point of Anglesey that faces the Snowdon Range. Now a Nature Reserve, it was a pilot-station then, guarded by its giant lighthouse. We slept and ate in the cottage of one of the pilots. Otherwise we were never under a roof for the whole of that enchanted August. In and out of the sea, exploring the rock pools, staring at the crimson sea-anemones shut, the pink sea anemones open, watching the greedy ways of the cormorants, collecting shells . . . A line by Dylan Thomas gives the whole unthinking bliss of that time—*Happy as the grass is green*.

A pen-friend wrote to me that *the cormorants are still on their rock and the cowries still plentiful*!

Can children, with beach-balls, blown-up rafts, grotesque rubber animals, know such happiness? I think so . . . But out of elements we did not know. . . .

Fragrant and golden-crested loaves emerged on the spade. I pointed out the ones I'd like.

Miss Mary Harris brushed her small hard-working hands off on her top-apron, and made out the bills, first Margaret's, then mine, on stray scraps of wrapping paper.

Mine was three shillings-and-eightpence all told. Three— or was it four? of those ambrosial loaves. Four buns. Two 'Chelsea buns', curled caterpillar-wise around themselves, 'varnished' the baker had said, with a little sugared water. They tasted nicer than any I'd eaten in Chelsea—or anywhere else.

IV

Besides these purchases there were two things I brought away from this morning-call at the Old Bakery. One was the scrap of odd conversation I'd had with a man—Casual help?

Friend of the Firm? Customer? All three, perhaps—who drifted in, came up to me and said he *knew* of me. (Not as an occasional broadcaster but as a professional story-writer.) And had read every word of my last thing aloud to his wife.

'Tell me, frankly, what you thought of it.'

'An interesting, non-sequent, collection of pieces about things you liked. What I liked best was about *you*. Your personal life, with your grandmother and so on.'

(*He could talk English, Lords, as well as we.* Better than most of us in fact.) 'Write some more about Wales.'

'Actually, it's what I'm trying to do at the moment . . . I can't find a title . . .' I told him a suggestion, half-jokingly, approved by my family.

'Call it nothing of the kind! Hurting people's feelings!'

'Well, what?'

'I will give the matter some thought,' he said. 'I will write to you. Goodbye now. Thanks for the pleasure.'

The second thing I brought away with me was the secret spirit of this old, this craftsman's place.

Most old places have one, if you listen.

Here (it told you), what other people in the catering-business put into their ultra-modern civilised equipment, into extra cleaning-staff paid to keep all surfaces like polished corners of the temple, and all floorspace constantly hoovered; into a sterilised spinsterly orderliness wherever you looked; into bright advertising slogans, lavish cellophane wrappings and a smart delivery van—these people of the Old Bakery put into the single purpose of making, in happy-go-lucky, old-fashioned surroundings, Good Bread that Tastes like Bread.

They win.

Chapter Seven
The Little Welsh Museum

I

An unusual example of the Old Order changing, to give place to the New, is to be seen at Tre'r'ddol.

This is on the turning away from the entirely modern big buttercup-yellow petrol station, on the road between Glandyfi and Aberystwyth. Look up the hill. You see that old-fashioned neatly sedate building?

It used to be a Wesleyan Chapel.

In 1961 it was bought, renovated and turned into a little Museum for mementos of a bygone Wales; the whole cost of this coming to £2,000.

Go up that path, through a graveyard less gloomy than most of them. There are none of those heavy, high, spiked iron railings. (I have never been able to fathom the reason for them!) Turf and flowers surround the few slate slabs (inscribed ER COF AM) beneath which forefathers of the hamlet sleep. The well-kept path leads to the open door.

You will be smilingly welcomed by Mrs. Jennie Jones, the trim and knowledgeable little lady in charge of the upper portion of the Museum.

You do not have far to look for traces of what it originally was. You see the solid oaken pulpit, but no steps to it. It stands level with the rows of pews. These have been repainted a defi-

nitely secular sky-blue, and are not for sitting on. They act as
supports for the vitrines or display cabinets. They keep from
dust or fingering many portraits and some ancient photographs of the Ministers who once preached, from that same
pulpit, sermons in Welsh, flavoured with the typical Welsh
hwyl, that dramatic rise-to-the-heights, fall-to-the-depths in-
tonation which often resounded through my own childhood.
For my Father liked, for the sake of the singing of the grand
old hymns, to attend Evening Service in Welsh. Often he took
me to Church with him. (I remember the solemn parson who
seemed, from the heights, to be shaking his finger straight at
us and intoning warningly: 'O, *Pechadur*!' (Sinners!) He
must have been of the calibre of a character in Richard
Llewelyn's *How Green was my Valley.* Do you remember the
poignant scene in Chapel where a miserable erring girl was
made to stand up before the whole congregation while she
was pointed out to hear the account of her sin thundered at
her by the Minister? She wept—or as the Welsh novelist more
graphically had it: 'She *bled* into her handkerchief.' Pitiless!
those days were past, I think, even before those of the ministers
portrayed in this Museum.

They—the portraits—are admittedly largely of men with
grimly implacable *Get-thee-behind-me, Satan!* expressions
but I have no doubt that their hearts were softer than the cut
of their jibs. Even if they invoked death and damnation as
threats for their congregation they may secretly have felt akin
to the gentle old mother of George Ponderevo in H. G. Wells'
novel *Tono Bungay* when she declared 'Oh, yes! I do believe
in Hell, George. I believe in Hell all right. But *I don't believe
anybody gets sent there.*'

Our own Mother, who was brought up more or less strictly
low C. of E. and to hold no brief for Non-conformists, used
nevertheless to admit that, 'Wesleyans are more like us.' I
don't know, by the way, what Non-conformists would have
thought of one of Mother's involuntary breakings out into
heterodoxy: 'You know, it's all the Same God, really!'

I noted one of the portraits is almost a conversation-piece.
Meticulously engraved, it represents the death of the prege-

thol. His sorrowing relatives have gathered about the bedside.
They are in shadow. He lies back on his pillows, brightly
illuminated, for, as you are meant to realise, Light Eternal
already shines upon him. His face is that of a mild and happy
Saint. Yes, but the message of the picture has been *felt,* and
set down by the Victorian artist with such obvious sincerity
that you could not laugh.

Laugh if you like at the collection in the next show-case of
Early-Nineteenth Century Valentines. Hands holding out bouquets of forget-me-nots, a shy swain in an incredibly choking
collar is posting an envelope containing one of these paper
lace-edged *billets* to arrive on February 14, eighteen- what?

My Nain had hoarded one such with the verse:

> *Beneath the Rose the Thorn is found,*
> *Beneath Love's smile the Dart.*
> *Oh, may his Arrows never wound*
> *Thy young and guileless Heart!*

Full, full was that Museum of other treasures. They were
of all dates from those coy Victorian Valentines back to the
oldest contribution; pieces of flint, arrow-heads picked up
from Bugeilyn, the fishing lake near Llanidloes. The row of
shining horse-brasses would be the envy of any collector.
There was a rich display of Welsh-lustre jugs, glowing copper-
lustre, gleaming silver-lustre. Water-colour views of this
County and that, appropriately framed, covered much of the
walls. Each exhibit was carefully labelled; its name inscribed
in beautiful, scholarly handwriting. There were busts in
glossiest Staffordshire pottery, of John Wesley, George Whit-
field, John Brynon of Caernarvon; also one of John Milton,
and, a little less expectedly, another of Mr. Keir Hardie
(given by Nicolas, Aberystwith.)

One-third of the treasures were gifts from those interested
in the Museum. I had this from Mr. J. R. Thomas of
Aberystwyth University, who was also my informant that the
remaining two-thirds were purchased by himself for the
Museum. Its running-costs—for lighting, heating, insurance,

fire-extinguishers, burglar-alarm system, and summer-season assistants' fees, were £300 annually, of which perhaps half is reimbursed by the contributions of visitors.

(Three hundred pounds . . . ? It gave one to think of the contrasting vast expenses that must be incurred by the upkeep of the British Museum, Victoria and Albert Museum, the Tate Gallery, the Wallace Collection. . . . Yet—I didn't for the moment know *why*, this modest little set-out around me seemed to have an unexplained something those other costly and established institutions *have not*.)

On a shelf behind glass I saw a row of handsome tall silver cups. I took them for trophies, prizes for scholarships or athletics—?

Oh, no. Those are Communion vessels, sent in from Wesleyan or Methodist Chapels. Small individual cups have superseded the Old Order. 'Because,' as Mr. Thomas had put it, 'of some silly hygienic fad.'

II

The lower portion of the Museum is reached by stairs difficult to negotiate except by the mountain-goat or the mountain young.

My sister had written a request about this.

So, that afternoon I was kindly allowed to enter by an outside door, usually kept locked.

On duty beside that door we found the custodian, Mr. Elwyn Edwards, brother to Mrs. Jennie Jones. He—a very-much-on-the-spot man with a sunburnt face, intensely alive and intelligent eyes, and in functional working-clothes—was polishing an old-time sickle to the brightness of the half-moon of which it had shape. He put it down, shook hands, and took us into the other lower rooms. Dark, after outside sunshine! until one's eyes grew accustomed to the non-lighting. Here, amongst other survivals, were farm-implements when such machinery as the tractor just *was not*. Of those forefathers of the hamlet who laboured on those country-farms one can only say, *They were stronger men than ours are, Gunga Din!*

Knee-high, ponderous-soled footwear they had! I don't know
how they managed even to lift one of those boots, let alone
wear that pair in which they would plod through the mud,
carrying those enormous wicker creels which in my ignorance
I took for lobster-pots. I learned that these were to hold peat.

'When I was a lad,' explained Mr. Elwyn Edwards, 'I'd
carry one of those, full of peat, on my back.'

He gave me a hard, brick-like sample of this fuel to hold:
then another, still moist. Everything was unbelievably *heavy*!
The vast kitchen-table, the bench beside it, at which farm-
people sat to eat.

One service for their meal was on show; a leaden plate—
not much bigger than a current afternoon-tea plate! A short,
sturdy horn-handled knife. A three pronged fork.

I looked about: It would not of course seem as dark when
it was less crowded with massive furniture …

'Candles? No. We had oil-lamps when I was a lad. That
lantern'—it was the size of the top of a pre-Neon London
Street lamp—'was for when we'd go out in the snow to dig out
the sheep.'

'I see you have the old grandfather clock,' I said, looking
up at the dim moon-like face a couple of yards above me.

'We have *five* grandfather clocks in the place,' said its
curator, proudly.

Suddenly—'Oh! There's a *harp,* too!' I exclaimed.

It had been a harp. It stood pushed into a corner. Just the
remainder of a harp. The ever-graceful shape. All strings gone,
but for one twist of wire that hung in loops about it.

'Is it a *delyn deiress*?' I asked, rather pleased with myself
for knowing. I'd picked up the name a week before.

'Yes, yes. It's the old Welsh triple harp. Have it re-strung?
Well indeed I believe it would be cheaper to buy one, which
would be a waste, too,' said the Guardian of relics. '*Not* the
same thing. This was given by Mrs. Browne Aberystwyth.'

Among the typically Welsh-type furniture I saw the
cwpwrdd tridard or three-tiered cupboard. We had a double-
tiered cupboard, which stood at Pantlludw. This one had no
initials, but it was dated 1741.

As we turned to go out, it was as though a woman had brushed against me.

I turned round and saw what I had missed when we came in.

From a stand, garments dangled like so many Bluebeards' wives.

'Those are the dresses ladies used to wear, once upon a time.'

Not crinolines. Heavy long gowns, skirts that could, as the saying was, 'stand alone'. My Nain was photographed in the midst of a skirt that could have achieved this standard. These were not of brocade or satin. The thick cloth stuff of them was made to last. Well, it had lasted. Sleeves and bodices were trimmed with sombre-coloured fringe that looked equally indestructible.

'This,' said the curator, taking up a rug-like fold and spreading it out—*Yards* of it! 'This was somebody's grandmother's wedding-dress.'

Nothing could have looked less like one. It was probably thought suitable for a Minister's bride at the time. No white nonsense for *her*! No filmy white veil over orange blossoms. The wearer of such a gown would have headgear to match. A bonnet, or a close-fitting toque would cover her hair and frame her young face. She would not be more than twenty-two. Older than our teenaged runaways who still defy control by dashing off by sports-car or motor-bike to Gretna. There would have been no necessity to make *her* a Ward in Chancery! She would have been brought up like her grandmother before her to have no ornament but that of a meek and quiet spirit and to submit herself to her husband. Otherwise she would not, could not have consented to being married in a gown of that deadly mud-brown?

A passionate heart may have thumped under that awful boned bodice. She may have been as radiantly happy in her lot as any Humanist in this permissive age. We shall never know.

On the way home I suddenly sensed why I'd had this special enjoyment while I was in that place, why more than I'd known when going through galleries of *objets d'art* in London, in Paris.

It was not just because I had Welsh blood that I so appreciated this little All-Welsh Museum. Something more imponderable had been about it. It was because here, in the unspoilable heart of Wales, these things *belonged*.

That furniture had made a typical Welsh home. Strings of that old damaged harp had vibrated under Welsh fingers. That tall clock had been heard to strike, that dress, those striped linsey-woolsey petticoats had been worn, those farm-tools had been used by forebears of men and women who *still lived in these counties.* They weren't marbles brought from a far and foreign land; not ornaments of gold reft from a Pharaoh's tomb. To me the Greek and Egyptian treasures of the British Museum always had a look of *loot.* These things we'd seen today were native to the soil (especially those boots! That peat-chopper!)

They had been given, chosen, or bought out of love. They were now cared for, cherished, shown with pride by people who knew and were part of their history.

So it is that in this Museum everything, from the flint arrow-head to the shining lustre-ware, gains from the fact that it has not been taken away from its own background.

What an illustration of the old maxim—

Drink the wine in the land that grew the grapes!

Chapter Eight
Welsh Concert

Do you look down upon those who 'try to keep up with the Joneses'?

Why! think what can be brought out of people by that Urge to Keep up, that driving Incentive, the force of Competition!

Take the Organisation to raise funds for the annual Royal Welsh Agricultural Show. Set for July of the summer of 1968 our County has—in *February*!—planned efforts to break the record set by 'the Joneses' of other counties.

Merioneth is to be this year's Hostess County.

—'And we so small, so poor compared with that Great Rich Cardiganshire. . . . All those Big Farms they've got . . . The University. . . . All those Wealthy People living there . . . !' was the situation.

And the reaction to it?

Emulation! *'Come on, Let's show them!'*

The note, struck by Colonel Williams Wynn, Lord Lieutenant of the County, President of the Show, supported by his gaily optimistic Lady was: *'We* can do it!'

Forthwith Merioneth flung itself heart and soul into things *In Aid Of*—. With, for a flying start, Llanegryn's Concert.

Llanegryn, 'Like little body with a mighty heart', is a small village with a large Village Hall.

Its full-sized stage has back-stage space to match. Space—blest factor!—for the neighbourhood's Silver Band. Space for the grand piano. Space, of course, for two harps to be brought in later . . . The premises would be 'for free' this evening. All performances would be a gift, all services too, would be in support of The Fund.

Other efforts all over the County were plans for Bring and Buy Sales, Farm house teas, Coffee-mornings, Wine-and-cheese evenings! A stall, enterprisingly 'with it' for hot dogs at the Outward Bound Sea School! A Grand Auction at the Camp; everyone canvassed to send treasures *or* junk from the attic! Garden fêtes, with Welsh handicraft and embroidered designs of Welsh emblems on sale! At Builth Wells, the Show itself has a Cinema presenting a documentary of Merioneth activities and scenery ('the film alone cost a thousand pounds to make!') On that day and in that place there would be the thrill of the Draw for the Guest Raffle organised by Miss Jane Williams Wynn of historic Peniarth, with six valuable prizes, all from Merioneth donors, to be won. Tickets a mere two-and-sixpence each for the *chance,* always within the bounds of possibility, of securing a Gorgeous New Car!—

I return you to Llanegryn.

The hall is planned to seat four hundred.

This evening it must give seats and standing-room for many more. It is filling up to overflowing, to bulging-of-the-walls, to condensation-of-moisture-on-the-floor-point before the final notes died away of what the programme puts as ANTHEM and we sit, after standing loyally for *The Queen.*

This *begins* concerts in Wales.

Announcements are made by a Chairman or, rather, Compère, born for the post of 'Life and Soul'.

Beaming enjoyment he faces the footlights, the blossoming

rows of primulas in pots, the crowded speckle of faces beyond, ready to break into laughter as soon as he opens his mouth.

Centuries back he would have been famous as Meuric the bi-lingual Jester who was wont to set the table in a roar at the Court of a Tudor King.

Here, and now, he is in charge of a programme with every item enthusiastically bestowed by enthusiasts with names— that I don't mention. It might be found invidious and certainly would run to lengthiness. . . . Christian and pre-Christian names that belonged by Tradition to a music-loving race.

The programme had everything. Much Welsh folk-song. Solos. Duets. Recitations. Ballads as in drawing-rooms of Yore. Believe it or not they included *The Lost Chord*.

Listeners as dated as myself, a sister and certain friends, were swept back to those lavish Concerts of the Nineteenth Century. Returned to Now-a-days by Choral-Speaking teams. One of these used the soft insistent accompaniment of Carl Orff percussion instruments. . . . No, this is not meant to be a report on items in correct sequence . . . It is a remembered mingling with that Spirit of Delight that so 'rarely, rarely' cometh . . .

What now?

A party of Towyn (Welsh spelling Tywyn) Grammar School boys and girls. Well-known to me was the sight of the brown-and-amber School uniform, striped ties, white stockings to mid-calf. Familiar sound was their let-loose-from-school racket as they bounded in and out along the corridor of what we named *the Parrot's Train,* between Towyn and Aberdovey, stopping at what used to be Gogarth Halt.

Here, tonight, these shouting rompers and chatterers were mute. Uniformed in shirts and blouses of pristine white. Drilled with movements as correctly simultaneous as a corps-de-ballet giving *The Parade of the Wooden Soldiers* they filed in on stage. Sat, in a row. Stood, in a row behind. All this at the unuttered words of command of their Genius-Teacher, from whom they never took their eyes. She raised a hand and drew forth melody.

E

With her back to the house, slim she was as the black body of a dragon-fly. She made you wonder how it could hold so much music. You could all but *see* the notes caught by her pupil's awareness as they poured, those notes, through her fluent conducting hands up, and out of her heart. 'Yea, her foot speaks', though not the language of Shakespeare's Cressida. Seven of her Chosen give the special composition by William Mathias of *Olwen* from the Mabinogian.

A surprise is the change to a German folk-song of which I know every note! It comes to me out of my receptive sixteenth summer in the Harz mountains. The Sunday Ausflug through the scent of the pine-woods, singing as we went!

> *Horch, was kommt von draussen 'rein*
> *Hola hi, hola ha!*

I could have wept tears of nostalgia over these tuneful echoes —'but let us not be too mushy', to quote my brother.

That Teacher-to-end-all-teachers had them as one pupil filing quietly off to the ample premises back-stage. Not a glance right or left as, in modest stillness and humility, they disappeared. Not a half-turn round. Not a half-smile to acknowledge the applause of the house, or even that there was a house. They might have been leaving the class-room.

There are two Schools of Thought as to the right Platform Manner.

For instance—

Beaming in added pleasure, Compère Meurig Rees had introduced the Star of the evening, the Celebrity of Screen and of Concert Platform—Richard REES. . . .

'Everybody asking is he a relative of mine! But no. No! Surname only. Reflected glory!' The compère drew back, and, smiling, the Star came on.

He had brought as his contribution to the first part of the Concert a Mozart aria and two encores—these last in the Welsh language.

Let musicians describe the voice of him, I shall not attempt
to do so.

Dramatic was the change to be seen now in the *presenta-*
tion of his art by a professional artist.

Every movement, of course, made it clear that on the stage
—any stage!—he was at home. There was more to it than
that, though. He was, intentionally, all that was hoped for,
expected of Local Boy who had Made Good. His look into the
excited house put it across that to him 'us people' meant as
much as would any packed audience at the Royal Festival
Hall, London. He *liked* to be here. He'd given thought to
pleasing us not solely by his singing but by his personality, his
appearance, his manner. The very cut of his extremely good
dark suit quoted :

'All for your delight.'

Delighted, the house would have been his before he had
given it a note.

'And now . . . Gifted family of our neighbourhood' was
proudly presented by the compère . . . 'Rectory, Llwyngwril !'

I had visited that Rectory some years back. The Rector had
given me material for one of my B.B.C. talks.

I hadn't on that occasion seen the sons of the Rectory.

Aged, as I judged, fourteen and eleven respectively, the
boys come quietly on. With faces no different from those with
which they would sit down at their school-desks, they take
their places, one at the Concert-harp, all elaborately decorated, the other at the Welsh harp of tradition, its frame un-
adorned but stately in stark simplicity. Each boyish head
reaches well under the top of the tall instrument that leans
against a slight shoulder. Hands not yet grown to adult
harping-size masterfully attack the strings.

The sound that came forth has 'done things' to me from
the first time I heard it. I was then a little girl, trotting along
to keep up with the long legs of Father, who had taken me
with him to visit the old gipsy harper in Caernarvon, was it?
Or Machynlleth? The flash-back shows only that it was in a
back-street, and that in a corner of a dark and stuffy kitchen
an old man sat with his queer instrument (the harp) laid on

his knees. Nursed, like a kitten? This was the first harp I had seen. I have never, in all my life, seen another like that one, and have since been told it must indeed have been old . . . Like *The Minstrel Boy to the War is gone with his Wild Harp slung behind him* was what I'd expected. . . . (Children of my age used, in those days, to know more poems than their Grown-ups ever heard from them.)

Father spoke, in Welsh.

The old gipsy-man said, 'Ie, ie.' I know that meant Yes!

He moved the harp on his knees. He clawed at it strongly with both hands. A loud sweet trilling came from the strings.

When Father on the way home asked if I'd liked that music, I only said, 'Yes.'

You couldn't tell a Grown-up that when that old man played, it had seemed—most extraordinarily!—to sound at the same time to be going on inside your own chest.

It's gone on like that for me. Whether in a London theatre when, through the overture, there steal a couple of phrases from the orchestra's harp; whether, at our Club's Welsh Section party, Telynores Gwendolyn Mason brings her lovely art to celebrate St. David's Day; even when, in a crowded street, traffic-noise has been threaded by the melodious strumming of some itinerant musician who had got his harp and his tin for money to the kerb, this has been my response.

(Some evenings later I listened to our 'special' harpist, Elsie Francis, 15, play for me, on her own harp, in her own home, and after eighteen months' study only of that loved instrument, the spirited Spanish piece which at the Eisteddfod in Aberystwyth had made her, as prize-winner, the second out of all Wales! From me it had won the tribute of a heart lifted, tears that nearly fell.)

So now.

Those boys play together, then one after the other.

The face of the younger one as he peered through the curtain of gleaming harp-strings might have been the face of a cherub looking through a shower of bright rain. . . . *'Loose Celtic analogy'* of which my husband had time and again accused me. How I wished that truly-musical Yorkshireman had been with me, listening !

Followed, a *Dawns y Glocsen,* a clog-dance. This is the Welsh form of the *Schuhplatler* danced by Tirolean mountain-lads. Often, in Tirol, I have watched them energetically stamping their loud rhythms on the cleared floor of the Achensee cafés. They wore their national kit of loose white shirt, gay 'White Horse Inn' braces, broad embroidered leather belts clipped their Lederhosen, and they had woollen knitted stockings, heavy shoes.

Less showily picturesque was the get-up of the Welsh boys just past childhood ! but that too was nationally traditional. Short jacket, short tweed knickers, rough woollen knitted stockings, heavy shoes. The cherub-through-the rain—how he would have resented that description !—now left the harp for centre-stage. He danced the Llanofer Reel to the harp-accompaniment of his brother. His stoutly shod, light feet were, like Olivia's, *pat to the music as its echo.* He gave then, *Dawns yr Ysgeb.* Dance of the Broom. Carrying it by a hand at each end of the broom-stick, the dancer skipped over it as nimbly as a cat, first to one, then to the other side. Is there a trace of ancient Welsh witch-craft ritual in this? For his finale he loosed the broom, does a hand-spring, stands on his head (a small cushion having been placed on the boards) and, keeping that position, he claps his feet together in perfect dance-rhythm up to the finish of the tune. Then—Head over heels ! Exit, right.

Warmly applauded, he did not reappear to take a bow.

Too soon it was the singing of the second Anthem. *Hen Wlad fy Nghadau* is the *end* of the Concert, in Wales. Now for the outward surge to the pack of cars, the coach for home. Some of the audience must still have been in that blissful after-the-show daze of not knowing if this were Thursday or Bryncrug.

As for me, the night rang with rippled harp-strings, with the rhythmic stamp of dancing clogs.

Next morning I wrote to Llwyngwril. Mrs. Oliver, asking for more.

Chapter Nine
Harpist and Clog-Dancer

I

On the date for which I asked, transport was supplied by the friend who drove on to make a long-planned water-colour sketch in 'Old' Llwyngwril, after depositing me at the Rectory. The picture, of windy March skies rioting high above the roof of a sturdy old stone cottage, was to be in due course accepted by the North Wales Group of the Federation of Art Societies and exhibited as 'Ty Gwyn' by Margaret Hayes.

A congenial and rewarding afternoon had been thus destined for each of us.

For at the Rectory I was welcomed in the spacious high-ceilinged Victorian drawing-room which was the living-room obviously 'lived in' by a musical family.

The two harps stood on one side of it. The piano was open: sheets of music on the rack. In a further corner a guitar lay on a chair. The atmosphere was of a home.

I sat in a red-cushioned seat by the fire, enjoying hot scones and tea, and 'gleaning' from the parents of those gifted boys.

'Not back from School yet. Be in presently,' said the Rector.

He is a pleasant, blond Celtic-type optimist from whom words come ungrudgingly about the subject in hand. This I remembered from that time I had a script to do for the B.B.C. He had kindly shown me over the small ancient Church of

Llangelynen, built by Irish missionaries close to the sea-marge below Llwyngwril. A holy-water stoup stands in its porch. He had told me the curious fact that this stoup was not man-made; it had been picked up on the beach already hollowed into its perfect shape by—who knows how many decades of the ceaseless action of the waves?

Later, I had heard that at the annual service in August this tiny Church is packed with visitors interested in the music for hymns and psalms being given solely on stringed instruments. Harp, and violin. How entirely appropriate that this should be the music of that Church! Just outside its porch door you may see the flat, worn slate tombstone of an itinerant harpist who in his day was known all over Wales: the King of the gipsies, ABRAM WOOD.

. . . 'Who plays for the Service? Why, those two boys. They're good. The sons of the Rector.'

Now the Rector was telling me :

'That old triple Welsh harp we have, the *Delyn Deiress,* the Llanofer harp, is two hundred years old.'

His wife, who is of the contrasting Iberian-Welsh type, and reminded me of a poppy, her head so dark against the bright scarlet of her jersey, took up with a smile as cheerful as her husband's

'Our boys learnt to play with the harp leaning on the *left* shoulder. The traditional way. Taught by Telynores Maldwyn, Nansi Richards.'

I knew the name of course.

'Isn't she one of the organisers of that Society—'

'Yes, yes! The Welsh Harp Society, Cymdeithas Telynau Cymru, they are trying to set up a workshop, imagine, there isn't one in Wales! for the repair and maintenance—Not to mention the manufacture of harps! They're so dear to buy, it's dreadful!'

'I know someone said it ought to be taught in every school in Wales. Was it she?'

'I daresay. She's the top-harpist in this county. Next time

she comes here I'll let you know. You must meet her.'

'I shall keep you to that, Mrs. Roberts.'

As for the care that has to be taken of these expensive instruments—'A draught is fatal. Any minute and—Ping! goes a string. And these little ones, look, eighteen pence each, and the big ones, up here, a pound to thirty shillings they cost. School-fees would go up if they *did* have them in every school! Yes, indeed. Cosseted like an Opera-singer they've got to be!'

Almost scared to stand too near these Lordly Ones, I moved.

'Your boys play the piano, too?'

'Oh, yes. They both have music lessons. At Towyn School. Very keen they are on music at Towyn.'

I saw on the piano scores of Bach, Schubert and the gaily coloured cover of *Mary Poppins*.

The Mother saw me look at this last and laughed.

'They have to know about all sorts, don't they? They have to be in with what's going on in the world!'

'Of course. And the guitar? Which of them plays that?'

'Both of them. Oh yes, they picked that up. Well, I don't really remember when.'

It came back to me how during one holiday among the mountains of Tirol, country so like Wales seen through a giant's magnifying glass! I had asked one of those friendly working-lads in Lederhosen, 'Who taught you to play?'

He'd look at me as if I'd asked him who taught him to speak. 'At home we can all play: all.' Adding, 'The guitar was always in the kitchen,' as if that made all clear. Music was in every breath of mountain air they drew. . . . So, here.

I asked Mrs. Roberts: '—and the recorder?'

'Oh yes. Both of them.'

'And who taught the younger one the Clog Dance?'

'I did,' said the mother with understandable pride. 'My father was a very good clog-dancer and his father before him.

In the family, you see.' Then she surprised me. 'That end of the *dawns y Glocsen,* you remember? As you saw it at the Concert? When he was standing on his head and clapping his feet in the air? Well, he, Gwyndaf, thought up that all by *himself*. His invention!'

She brought out and showed me a couple of pairs of the clogs.

'These are Dutch, of course.' They were of light coloured wood with turned-up toes. Sabot-type. The other pair had stout black leather uppers, doorstep thick soles . . . In these the boy had danced effortlessly, and—but for the loud metronomic sound of tap-tap on the platform boards—like a wave o' the sea.

'They're not as heavy as you'd think, from the noise!'

I'd been told so by Father's friend the Clog-maker all those years ago.

This nice man had turned up at Esgair with a cart, a roughly-made tent of sack-cloth, poles, tools, to ask leave to pitch his tent—'Down there by the stream, where the alder-tree's down. . . . I'll pay for the wood. It's for the clog-*soles,* you see, sir. I've this contract for so many. Only the soles. The leather uppers are done by some firm. A lot they have to get for the factory-workers in Manchester. Yes! it's like thunder first thing in the morning when those girls in their clogs are off along the streets to work.'

Will you think of the difference in the way of life of the crisply-shod factory-employees of Now?

Father, always interested in the work of men's hands, halted at the Clog-maker's pitch many times during the next week, to ask how he was getting on, to watch, to comment.

When this craftsman went, leaving small neat heaps of light sawdusty chips to be scraped up into baskets and taken for the kitchen fire, we all of us missed him. We were glad he'd said he would come again next year.

How long is it since his craft has become a thing of the Past, or mechanised?

'And your boys, Mr. Roberts, when they leave school . . . ?' Rather nervously I brought out the question. 'When they're grown up, are they to be professional musicians?'

Both parents laughed aloud.

'No indeed!'

'Nothing like that!'

'Electronic engineering! That's what they've set their hearts on, the pair of them. Absolutely!'

'And Gwyndaf—*He's* determined to be a pilot as well. . . . You should see that boy's bedroom. Just one mess of little paper model aeroplanes!'

What a relief.

Not to run the risk of becoming spoilt, vain, jealous of any fellow-artist's better Press, higher fees? *Not* professional musicians, full of what was once known as the D.A.T. (Damned Artistic Temperament), a trial in the home and to the wife? Good!

Illogical. *Must* a professional musician mean that? Hadn't one of our best men-friends been a pianist, dynamically musical to his finger-tips, well-known at London concerts, well-paid also, and sought after for 'Society' parties—and hadn't he remained completely without 'frills'? He, Jack Phillips, professionally Ivan Phillipovsky, once told me that when, for 'hostilities only' he served as a submarine officer, he felt for the first time that this was a *full* life . . .

Fortunately it had not taken a War to give these Roberts boys ambitions apart from the world which they could still serve as highly-gifted amateurs. They would be men 'in the round'. But—Electronic Engineering?

It sounded alarmingly complicated. Men went up to the Universities to study the many branches of it. To me it was Greek—worse! mathematics . . . I made enquiries later, and was given 'words, words' . . . Power transmission, problems in the design of electrical machinery . . . The reduction of acoustic noise . . . Ah. Would that have to do with my recurrent dream of an aircraft silent in flight? . . . Control systems and electrical power networks. . . . Help!

II

The boys came in quietly.

Typical rather than special. Expression on their young faces—(*Tea?*)—changed to the guarded expressionlessness of schoolboys finding a visitor.

Their mother said,

'This is Mrs. Oliver who's come to see us.'

Politely they shook hands.

Young-feeling, hard, cold from the March wind outside this warm room. Not yet full-sized hands that could already call out such melody and would later set in motion such (to me) unintelligible machinery . . . They stood. Between us rose an invulnerable barrier: *Silence*. It seemed minutes that they stood mute as the two untouched harps. Weren't they going to play . . . or even utter?

I said as if to grown artists but more diffidently,

'I liked your playing so much. At the Concert.'

Their mother caught my glance of appeal and put in cheerfully,

'Play for *Mrs*. Oliver, boys.'

They moved to the harps. Sat. The room filled and thrilled to the music of the Llanofer Reel that they had given at the Concert.

It died away like a sigh.

I cleared my throat and said, 'Lovely.'

They gave me a polite look.

They didn't utter.

Could they be—were they shy?

I was, I can tell you. Petrified. For suddenly I'd seen these two Grammar-school boys as what they indubitably were. Force-in-bud. Inheritors to be of *Regions Caesar never knew* —or that anybody else knows, for that matter yet. These boys would be skilled men in that New Era of which we are given alarming hints, prophecies. Now in a broadcast by a responsible professorial Reith lecturer, now in the publication of startling scientific discoveries by young, confident Nobel prize-winners.

How can we foresee what further revolutionary activities may harness the Electronic engineering on which boys set their hearts? What undreamt-of Speeds? What closer contacts with Outer Space?

I, from whom old Charon leaning on his oar awaits his pence, knew only that these half-grown boys I saw would, as men, be among those who aim to '*put a girdle round about the earth in forty minutes*'. (The record is still held by Puck of Athens.)

The boys rose. Half turned towards the door. (*Tea in the kitchen?*) It was to be exactly their exit into the wings after their items at the Concert.

'Oh . . . I'd—' I held out modest gifts I'd brought—and forgotten. Chocolates for each; for each the traditional minstrel's fee of a silver coin. I handed them to the elder, David, first.

They stood, unwrapped the packets.

They *uttered*! With what stony politeness.

'Thank you.'

'Thank you.'

They looked down to read what I had written on the wrappings of the coins.

FOR THE HARPIST.

FOR THE CLOG-DANCER.

Boys, not girls, are the mysterious sex. For then—Why *then*? Unpredictably both looked straight up at me and gave me what they hadn't given to their audience from the concert-platform at Llanegryn—a very nice and natural smile.

Chapter Ten
Roadsters' Refuge

I

You, if you are a visitor to our neighbourhood, may have passed the place? The tall, pale-façaded, three-storied building just off the road from Aberdovey to Towyn, on the left-hand side as you go towards Towyn Hospital?

But did you hear its queer name—'Escuan'—and what it means? Did you know the queer, almost medieval condition on which the farm is still held? *No man who went in at its gate and asked shelter for the night was to be refused.* Any tramp was certain of finding refuge here.

Ancient custom surviving modern usage always fascinates me.

I wrote to the present owner of the place (that same Meurig Rees who had so ably compèred the Llanegryn Concert) asking 'permission to view' and if I might be told something of the tradition.

His wife wrote hospitably back and suggesting a date.

Now the entrance to the big farmhouse was the first of several surprises.

That pale, tall, narrowish façade was only a side of it: its front was of native grey granite, facing a wide cobbled space. (The farm-yard itself to the right as you went in, was spacious, with big sheds.) Cobblestones of the approach were blessedly easy to walk on; small, flattish, and oval. The usual lean, black-and-white, sharp-muzzled sheep-dog lay on the lowest of the short flight of steps leading to the front-door. His clever eyes gave me a once-over, and closed again as his mistress came out in greeting.

Mrs. Rees, slender, frocked in well-fitting corn-flower blue, brunette, and smiling, was the sort of woman with whom one can get on at once.

She led me through a kitchen replete with amenities that previous owners of farmhouses, however big, had never possessed, into a large living-room where Past joined Present in amicable co-existence. The further end of it was made by a sweepingly curved bow-window giving on to the prospect of Cardigan Bay . . .

'Escuan' roughly translated meant 'Look-to-the-Sea'. 'Yes, we put that window in ourselves. We haven't finished all we are going to do to Escuan, still.'

Prosperity was the note of this home. Not 'jumped up'. Worked for! Justifiably delighted in.

She wheeled in the tea-trolley; it shone with silver bright as her own face. Delicious sandwiches. A cream-layered cake that meant effort to refuse.

We chatted, and I seemed to have known her, always! Before she was married, too. She was 'from these parts'. Her people were farmers. Her sisters had married farmers.

'Yes! we're a real farming family. All of us. Always working in or about the farm. I can't imagine doing anything else! It's been my life.'

She didn't look even the number of years she said she'd lived. She made it sound the right life to live. She was saddened, though, by the difficulties facing today's young married couples who want to buy a farm.

'The least they'd have to give for one of any size is ten thousand. A small farm—well, the owners wouldn't want to part, would they? And to start and build a farm of their own, oh dear,' she went on as she plied me with more tea, 'and you *will* taste my scones I made for you?—To *think* of all the new farm-machinery and equipment that *must* be provided . . .

Oh, it's all so much more difficult than it was in my father's
and my grandfather's time for the young people . . .'

'So, what will the young do? All rush to College and white
collar jobs, *teaching,* do you think?'

'I suppose so,' she said; obviously considering it was not so
rewarding a future for her own young daughters.

She had three of them. Two of them were already at Doctor
William's Dolgellau, the best Welsh girls-school in the country. The youngest was due to go there in the coming term.

One of the others was worried over her recent School
report. Her headmistress was bewildered because, though her
term work was very good, her work in exams was below it.

'Term work is all right,' the girl had said, 'but oh! as
soon as I get into that examination-room—*everything goes
BLACK!*'

—Flash-back to that same phenomenon at St. Winifred's
School in Bangor days, when, upon anything to do with the
accurséd subject *Arithmetic* there had fallen upon me the
plague of Egypt *'a darkness that could be FELT.'*

II

Enter Mr. Meurig Rees, less ebulliently than upon the concert platform, but with the gaiety of the compère still alive
behind the cordially social manner of the master of the house.

While still at tea ('Look at me! My wife tells *me* not to put
on weight whatever I do and the same time she's making me
cakes like this!') he began to give me the information for
which I'd asked.

'Yes, yes. The original condition—*No refusal to any man
who asked for a night's lodging*—Still there! In my father's
time we had all these roadsters—we got to know them well,
the "Regulars". They'd come up to the front, ask for the
lodging, leave their box of matches—That was the only
danger, *fire!*—My father would put the matches down on
our kitchen-table, and in the morning they'd come up, and
take back their matches and be off on the road again.'

Almost feudal it sounded. Except that there'd be no

matches. Some other token would have been evolved.

'Did they have a meal here, Mr. Rees?'

'No. It was part of their custom—their *code* that they had
—not to require it from us. They went to a farm further on
for food, if they hadn't some in their bundle, or bag. Only
thing they asked from us was hot water to brew their tea.
They gave us very little trouble. None, really. The only disturbance was the noise of quarrelling, sometimes, among
themselves.'

'What about?'

'Oh, if a new-comer pinched some corner of the shed that
was a Regular's pitch. Either that, or having shown a naked
light in the place. The most quarrelsome fellow we had was a
Canadian, Tom Moon. Been a soldier. You could see that;
drilled, you know. Held himself very erect. *Arrogant!* . . . If
a new man so much as looked towards Tom Moon's claim to
his corner of the shed, we'd hear the row from the house all
night.'

'I suppose the others all talked in Welsh?'

'Curiously little Welsh you'd hear talked. Most of them
came from Shropshire way, Hereford way. Over the border.
And, of course, it was seasonal—their coming.'

'Like the swallows.'

'Exactly, except that it was in the winter. They wouldn't
mind sleeping out in the open in the summer. Lots of them
would like it better. But in the winter we'd have twenty a
night, asking. Twenty a night, often! You must remember,
Mrs. Oliver, that this was in my father's time. I was a young
lad to start with. They made great friends with me. I talked
with them, knew many of them, well. Then they dwindled.
Then we didn't see them again.'

'Oh! Why?'

'Thirty-nine! The War and the call-up.'

'Of course. But afterwards?'

'The last real roadster came here some years ago now,' said
the owner of Escuan. 'An oldish man, tired out. Sad, that.'

III

He took me out to show me 'the site' where they were put up.

Down the shallow steps that those happy wanderers had gone up to leave their matches on the kitchen table, across the cobbles, and beyond into the spacious farmyard that was divided from the main road by sturdy heavily-cemented granite walls.

He pointed at them.

'Somewhere in there, I believe, is where they put their "Mark",' he said. 'Oh, yes, of course, our regular roadsters left a mark, I know; to show their pals who came by that this was the place. I know. But they'd none of them tell me where it was, and I've never found out where, *or* what.'

'Gipsies,' I said (having heard this from Nain), 'sometimes leave twigs in a certain shape by the road-side.'

'Roadsters, I fancy, cut their sign in the cement before it was dry. I'll never know. Here's the shed.'

More sizeable than I had expected! Long, high-roofed under beams. With partitions.

'We've had to build on quite a bit. Calves, over there.' There was a stirring at the dim further end. 'You know, as my wife told you, we can't afford to sell milk any more. Preposterous it sounds?—Still, one-third of this space is what the roadsters had.'

It was obviously sufficiently roomy.

'Partitions here. Mattresses were of bracken from the hills, with sacks over.'

I remembered Father telling us that almost the most comfortable bed he'd known had been up in the Peiwar, during the Afghan War of 1878. It had been made of springy Himalayan heather, and his servant had cut a fresh lot every morning to re-make his bed.

'In the spring,' said Mr. Rees, 'we took all the old bracken mattresses and the sacks that had seen service all winter and piled them into one big heap in the farmyard, set fire to them and burnt 'em to ash.'

F

Glorious blazing Beltane bonfires!

'You'd many hands, of course, for that.'

Mr. Rees laughed.

'On the morning that they knew we were planning to make the fires—Amazing how early they were awake! Nothing the roadsters wouldn't do for the farmer—except WORK! They left that to the novices. They'd up and gone!'

We stood talking in the shed that had once reverberated to voices quarrelling, or hummed with voices friendly, discussing the state of the roads—

'And of the world, sometimes,' said Mr. Rees. 'I've been surprised what a lot of quite serious, thoughtful philosophising I overheard going on here. A few of these chaps came from decent homes, you know. Some of them told me they were the black sheep of good old families. It could well be true.' He twinkled suddenly, broke off, 'I must tell you about our road-ster who was watching a road-man at work. Near our gate, it was. He was working, working, trying to split a big piece of granite, hammering at it for all he was fit, bang, bang! no use, couldn't shift a splinter, BANG—The roadster goes up to him. "Hey, you don't seem to be doing much about that, mate; let me have a try."

'He takes the hammer. One sharp tap to the granite and it falls neatly in two.

'The road-worker stares. "Lordy! *I couldn't*"—

' "Ah, you were at the wrong College, mate," says our chap. "College where I learnt the knack I was six months at it!" '

'In clink, of course'—for what misdoing? I wondered. Nain had her own peculiar standards about that. I'd heard her say, 'There is *stealing* and there is *taking*; a different thing.' Although a landowner herself she was (gipsyishly?) indulgent towards poaching. That was *taking,* and a sporting risk. But picking-pockets was *stealing*. A pick-pocket was *mean*.

'Mr. Rees! Have you ever missed anything?'

'Never, NEVER. They might have done anything, anywhere else. But not here. That was the Code. Nothing said about it, but that was it. We gave them this. They gave us that.'

'I see.' I liked it. Why isn't there more of that kind of trust in the world?

'I'd a man here once who went sick **on me.** We weren't able to do anything for him here. I rang **up the** workhouse infirmary at Dolgellau—he was pretty helpless, destitute; they said they'd send an ambulance. Which they did. Before they came he handed over his old bag to our waggoner. Asked him to keep it for him; when he was well he'd call in here again and pick it up. "Open it after I've gone and check it if you want to," he said. When the waggoner opened it there was twenty-five pounds in it! You see? He didn't want the workhouse infirmary to get that. If they knew there was that money on him they'd charge him for his keep. He considered it was *his* money, and he was going to have it kept safe for him. So he handed it over to the farm's waggoner, knowing that he'd see every penny of it back; as he did, of course.'

'I hope he gave a tip to the waggoner.'

'He might have done. That was between the waggoner and him.'

'Then there was one of these kind I was mentioning before, who could talk on quite serious subjects, intelligent, evidently had been a bit of a reader, though he looked—And his *clothes* . . . ! Well, he and the man he was tramping with were buddies who'd talk together for hours, equally ragged and disreputable, didn't give a hoot for anyone else. One morning he said,

' "Look, we'll go up over there for a bit of breakfast," pointing to that farm up the hill.

' "No, we won't," says the pal, "I been there. People aren't co-operative."

' "I'll go, then," says the more high-brow one. "I'll get round them."

' "You're welcome to *try,*" says the pal. "I'll wait by the side of the road for you. I bet you won't be long!"

'He sat. Waited. And waited. Finally a neat young woman in an apron came down with a tray of refreshments "with the compliments of the master of the house".

' "*Gor!* Pretty nice of him I must say. . . . But hold on a minute, Miss, I go shares with my mate, him that went up to the house, where's he got to—?"

' "He's the master," says the maid.

'This *happened*,' said Mr. Rees. 'I know it sounds like a magazine story. It happened. There are—or were—these people who have homes, relatives who'd look after them, even money of their own. . . . They go off on the road.'

'Why do they?' But I'd guessed before he spoke.

'It's the Lust of the Road. It drives them. They want to feel free, not have anything to do with a settled, routine life. They don't want to know what's going to happen next day; they can't *do* with worthy respectable stay-put people, they want associates that have more *colour*; they gang up with others like themselves, stick to them or leave them when they choose, here today and gone tomorrow. That's the life! Or was. . . . There's no place for them in our present society,' said the man who had made friends with roadsters, rather sadly. 'Things have changed too much. There are pensions, funds, welfare-work, homes of various kinds. All sorts of things are given to people, now, that never used to be. Sometimes, do you know, I can't help feeling nostalgic about the old ways. Some of them, that were—'

I asked him what he thought about all the rebellion and delinquency which is now so much discussed, the utter lawlessness, the deterioration—so much and so deplored!—of the young people of today. 'Are they so much worse?'

'They seem so, to the older generation, don't they? But as to *being* worse . . . They've got to have an outlet. There isn't the scope and there's too much. There aren't the rules against more harmless mischief any more—and they've got to have the outlet. That's why they break out into wrecking railway carriages and throwing bottles at football matches . . . and having scraps with policemen . . . and worse. We got into mischief but not that kind. They'll simmer down. Plenty of young scamps have.'

'I know,' I said, 'but these Reformed Rakes don't seem to remember what they've *been*? They've lost sympathy with the young. So the young don't bother to have sympathy with any older generation—'

'Oh, come.' His face was suddenly that of the compère who cajoled his audience at the Llanegryn Concert. He laughed. 'You and I,' he said, kindly inclusive, 'don't do so badly at understanding the young!'

I took leave of this couple of delightful new friends.

Through the gate which had in its time admitted that jesting jail-bird, those 'Regulars', Tom Moon the pugnacious Canadian, the sick man who could entrust the bag with all his money to the farm's waggoner, and the rest of all those hard-heeled weary wanderers who had sought and received their night's lodging at Escuan, we passed out to the open road.

Flash-back to Victorian times—

In softly gas-lighted, plumply-cushioned drawing-rooms ladies wearing evening-dress of that date would sit and listen, thrilled, to the sentimental ballad—which an inappropriately white-waistcoated baritone warbler trolled forth—

> *Homeless, ragged and tanned*
> *Under the changing sky!*
> *Who so free in the land,*
> *Who so con-TENTED—as I?*

Say what you like—Many a true word was set to these mushy old tunes!

Chapter Eleven
On Having Fun

I

'Don't get old, love,' said my little white-haired Yorkshire mother-in-law. 'There's no fun in it.'

I was newly-married and never considered Getting Old as a thing that could happen. To other people, yes. To myself, never. I laughed.

'How'd you stop it, Mam?' I could call her by the Welsh name; she liked Wales, and I liked her.

Her advice—'Take care of your health, and don't give way to serious thinking.'

In my own off-beat way I have taken care.

I've avoided poisons, by which I mean cigarettes, 'tranquillisers', and dope by all its names. Tea and coffee? They *are* drugs. . . . Still, as I've been used to them from my youth up, I'm immune. Like Mithridates. I've followed Shakespeare's *Throw physick to the dogs, I'll none of it*— Except when it's offered by those whose opinion I respect.

I subscribe to Mr. Kipling's *Every green thing that grows out of the mould was an excellent herb to our Fathers of old.*

No hat—or scarcely ever—for me. No muffling-up, in spite of cries of 'Put something warm round your neck, do!'—or, more Welshily, 'SHUT your coat!'

Until I was well over eighty I never missed my daily dip, summer or winter, in cold water whether of sea, river, or lake. While I was 'London-Welsh' this meant that in sweater and any old skirt over my swim-suit, I scampered from Willow Road across Hampstead Heath to Kenwood Pond. This place, though near enough to where you could get views of the dome of St. Paul's Cathedral looming like a grey soap-bubble through the morning mist, might have been a hundred miles away from any town.

Fringed with willows, rushes, reeds, yellow iris, wild mint, it was shared by water-fowl and a kingfisher. 'In those days a roughish wooden shack was our dressing-shed. A narrow plank platform with wooden steps led down to the water. Guardian of the pool was Mrs. Lilian King, the life-saver, a fine swimmer from a line of swimmers and divers, and the mother of a boy, Bert, who has inherited the family tradition. It is good to have known her and the other water-fans. What fun we had during those gay early mornings in the one and only true Democracy I've ever struck.

'Class' just was not. Only that spice of life variety. An elderly German Baroness, young housewives, office-workers, Sylvia the stage-dancer, a girl called Limehouse Lil—we were as one in the free-masonry of the All-the-Year-Round-Water-cult. We respected as well as liked 'Our Kingy.' She is one of the unforgettables. I can still hear her cheery calls across to the further bank. And when it was: 'That's enough! You come on in now, you Berta!' in I came.

During a long-ago frosty December several of us were ice-breakers. 'Zeroines' according to some humorist. Heavily-overcoated young Gentlemen of the Press came to report this scene. They called through the shut door of the shed where we were getting into our Club-costumes: 'Hurry up, ladies, please! *We're* on a cold job!' They sent our star, Sylvia, back twice to the diving-plank to repeat her 'turn' while they stamped snow off their boots and applauded. Their leave-taking line was, 'Well, goodbye, girls! Your boy-friends will spend Christmas going to inquests!'

From the airport I was rung up. Furious pilot's call of

'Ma! I saw it in the *Daily Mirror*. I FORBID it, Ma.'

I laughed.

Kingy and I still write to each other for anniversaries. We exchange notes on grandchildren, news of Sylvia, still diving or sunbathing on her hacienda in Latin America, about the 'Changes, Berta, since the Good Old Days at the Pond, where we had fun, didn't we?...'

Some of the best fun—almost—that I've ever known.

As to 'serious thinking'? There are plenty of people who are good at it. Aren't there also plenty of other, gayer if superficial aspects of Life?

My job was to try to convey these. Encouragement has come by hearing that my stories cheered wounded soldiers and other patients in Hospitals. Even more prized by me is this tribute to my *genre* as a writer. The report that my novels were eagerly sought-after, by those unhappier ones of earth, in the libraries of *prisons*.

II

'Time is against ladies'? True, that ill-conditioned old Baldie with the Hour-glass has scythed away much of the unthinking gaiety—Not all! in spite of my Welsh grandmother's warning, 'Berta, because she doesn't play cards, is laying up for herself a Miserable Old age.'

'I'd be worse miserable if I *did* play cards! They're like arithmetic to me, Nain.' Blankly I stared at the unintelligible spread of playing-cards, dotted black or red, laid out on the square green table by the long diamond-latticed drawing-room windows. This was in Nain's old home Pantlludw, scene of so many of our holidays. 'It's the worst part of School—I simply can't get *on* with anything to do with numbers or figures.'

'Fie! You should learn.'

'I can't.'

'Fiddle-de-dee.' One of the expressions from her Quaker

schooldays. 'You don't try . . . You will be sorry, later,' said Nain, shaking a warning head.

Other Grown-ups of her age at that time wore caps like a blanc-mange with a stiff black bow high in front. Nain wore an unusual short mantilla of Limerick lace adorned by a large flat rosette. It framed her face and her swept-back side-wings of silver hair. Her shawl of softest black silk, fringed, added to the effect of her being in a curiously becoming fancy dress as an Old Lady. Rings sparkled on her fingers as her hands, not small but shapely and deft, shuffled the cards. She would inveigle anybody (not me!) into a round game. Sons! visitors! grandchildren! When my sisters looked too little to have anything to do with cards except to play with the mother-of-pearl whist counters, round or fish-shaped, that lived in Nain's red lacquer bowl, she taught them *Beggar my Neighbour*.

Three of the girls grew up to have no time for cards. The fourth, Ursula, became a keen Bridge player. I remained unteachable about numbers whether on cards or an Arithmetic examination-paper.

Nature, abhorring that vacuum, filled up the gap. How? With a retentive memory for verse. Verse, deathless or doggerel. I can have it played back for me, by that silent virtuoso Imagination, just as the current generation can put its rave-records on the gramophone. It's been as much fun for me as it is for them to listen to the latest Top Ten. It's also been my solace through life.

On one occasion it has brought actual physical help. This was when I was on Woman's assignment of bringing a child into the world. Struggling . . . In those days we were not yet instructed in pre-natal cultural exercises. Instinct told me to use the force of Rhythm. Strong Pagan verses I had by heart. . . .

> '*Mithras, God of the morning, our trumpets waken the Wall!*
> *Rome is above the nations, but Thou art over all.*'

I repeated aloud and :

> '*Many roads Thou has fashioned—all of them lead to the Light!*'

Again, again it helped.

Later, the nurse with my new son in her arms said, 'Are you a Roman Catholic, dear?'

'No. Why d'you ask me that?'

'Because only Roman Catholics seem to know such lovely hymns to say instead of crying out when they're in labour.'

Well! *It's all the same God,* as Mother once (imprudently!) affirmed.

(Mithras . . . !)

I ventured to write a line of acknowledgement to my most revered poet.

Mr. Kipling wrote back in his own hand that he was specially glad about 'the hymns' which made him feel proud.

As to you card-addicts whose fun it is to sit for the whole of a lovely summer afternoon, *clamped* to that green Bridge table indoors when the sun is on the roses outside—Will your Old Age be free of all misery?

Will there be no searing frustration when, with good cards in your hand, you've been landed with a poor partner? And what about your feelings when you yourself are considered a handicap? I've been told that some of you enthusiasts were actually *forced to give up playing* because of the 'Post-Mortem' —the vindictive discussion, after the game, of how defeat had been brought about . . . Whereas, if only So-and-So had played the—etc. It was more than you could take.

You're left . . . Your occupation, like Othello's, gone? So much fun out of your life? Poor you.

Nain wasn't a bit like that.

A good game of cards was to her a pastime. I've heard her laugh merrily over the unexpectedly crafty winning of a trick by the opposing grandchild. 'Ah, serpent! *Serpent!*'

At the end she would gather up the pack with the same bright look on her face whether or not she'd had any luck.

She had *fun*.

What is your personal idea of Having Fun?

There's nothing on which tastes differ more wildly.

But yours—? Would it be climbing icy Alpine heights at the risk of your life (and that of your rescuers)? Or relaxing at your ease in your own private comfortable sound-proof library, your sole companionship being books? Or hearing yourself acclaimed by the hurricane of shouts as you finish— first!—in a closely-contested Grand Prix? Or gambling among the Top Names in a glittering Continental Casino? Or (least understandable of all, to me) letting yourself down, alone, into the dark depths of earth, pot-holing?

Lucky people need not depend upon any specific brand of enjoyment. They can find it in anything, anywhere. Like our Welsh Grandmother. Nain, if anybody, could 'draw honey from the weed.'

In her earliest girlhood she must have tasted Life as something so honey-sweet—Here, if you will forgive me? I'll break a thread.

Nain's adolescence has a flavour so different from that of the young American writer Tom Wolfe's record of 'the mad hilarity' that seeps through the way of life of the mod, hippie, and 'in' young people, that it should have space to itself.

May I show you, mostly in her own words, something of her own youth?

III

FUN IN AN OLDER WALES

> *Bliss was it in that dawn to be alive*
> *But to be young was very heaven*

—lines which seem to some a crass over-statement but were, I think, a truth to Nain, my Grandmother, in Wales.

Her childhood was 'made', I believe, by two factors, one of which stayed by her and supported her through the rest of her life.

She, little Mary Anne Mathews, was the only girl, with three brothers. The youngest, John, died as a baby. But the two other boys, Oliver and Richard, were for her the greatest friends and good companions. Their father had died young. He was thirty-eight—his little daughter seems to have known him only as the Shadow whose passing away had clouded their Mother's life.

'I was fonder of my grandmother at Esgair than I was of my own Mother,' she admitted to me once. 'My Mother was always *sad* . . .' May this have left the boys and the little Miss more freedom? Together they went about finding birds' nests in the wooded grounds of Esgair or Pantlludw. Together they explored the countryside, scrambling up hill and down dale. They invaded Pantlludw's kitchen . . .

Time and again one has heard how children have always liked being in a kitchen and have preferred kitchen company to the society of their own Grown-ups.

Why is this?

My life-long Irish friend ('Toddie' of my Slade-student days) said, 'Ah, it was because there was always interesting work to watch *going on* in a kitchen and servants were easier to understand and were more tolerantly kind.' That's true, I think.

In Pantlludw's warm and homely kitchen, where hams and sides of bacon dangled from hooks in the ceiling, little Miss (according to her own journal of bygone days written for her grandson Bernard) played tricks on 'dear old Betty' who appears to have taken it with perfect good humour, even when the child came up softly behind her, then leapt unexpectedly off the kitchen table on to her back. (*What* I, hating to be taken by surprise, should have done to the *evil* little practical joker!) Betty merely went on producing good foods that they, with the taste-buds of the under-tens, greedily enjoyed. The journal gives the recipe for a favourite Sunday dish.

Listen to this, ye followers of Freud in Sunday Illustrated Supplements! ye who pride yourselves upon *taking trouble* over the preparation of food! Old Betty (who quite likely could not read) *put Oat-cake to the fire till it was quite crisp. Then crumble it and place a layer in the bottom of a bowl. Then a layer of white bread, cut thin. Then mashed potato. Repeat these layers until the bowl is full, when you pour over it a strong broth made from hanging, broiling beef* (the beef was for Sunday dinner) *or mutton.*

Think of the time and care involved, you to whom broth (soup, you'd call it) means INSTANT processed powder factory-fresh from the tin, no worry barring hot water to pour on to it!

'This was a winter dainty,' records the journal, 'and each Sunday the good old woman' (Betty) 'rejoiced our childish hearts by sending a little basin to us. It used to arrive before we were up and was the signal for me to rush into my little brothers' room to claim my share.'

Would you see any childish hearts of Now being rejoiced over this 'mush' for breakfast? Yet, how much more health-building for childish bodies than are these lurid pink iced 'lollies' on sticks, as sucked by even their bearded Grown-Ups. (In my view, ice is at its best when it forms lovely icicles to hang from the rocks; and the only place for a beard is on Father Christmas.)

Mary Anne's eldest brother Oliver, 'loved by the Gods', was drowned when he was fourteen while bathing in the deep pool of the River Dovey at the curve not far from Dovey Bridge.

She and her brother Richard remained inseparables . . . 'and after about eight years of age no word of anger ever passed between us.'

Entries later describe her 'sharing in most of his pursuits.'

. . . When he shot snipe on the hills I walked with him,

and on one occasion the cold was so great that my dress, wet in the bogs, froze around me like a hoop. When a brook was too broad for me to cross over, he carried me over.

. . . He was three years my senior, a dark handsome man of six foot-two-and-a-half inches, with the kindest, most gentle nature that ever blessed a strong man. . . .

In the house of my youngest sister there is a picture of this Great-Uncle Richard of ours, sitting on the hill above his home Pantlludw with the unchanged view of the Dovey winding away in the distance. At his knee fawns the inevitable black-and-white sharp-muzzled sheep dog. His face, curiously enough, might be that of a currently 'in' young man because of the uncropped dark locks and the small side-burns. A looker, certainly, decide his great-nieces, impartially.

The journal :

Some of his friends still remember him as the finest man they have ever seen. . . . He went out to California at the time of the Discovery of Gold in that country with his friend, Mr. Edward Maitland, who wrote a book called *The Pilgrim and the Shrine* in which there is a description of him (Richard) as 'The Major'. He died a few months after his arrival in the country, of a kind of influenza then prevalent in the colony.

Elsewhere his sister writes :
'Of my brother Richard, dead these forty years, I cannot write without pain.'
He had brought out of her the *faculty* of deep affection. And he had in common with her the second thing which had made her childhood, youth, and indeed the rest of her life happy—*Nature she loved.*

Her journal:

> There was a group of oaktrees near the bend of the drive
> at Pantlludw which we children used to call 'my three
> brothers and me'. It is sacred to me by that name, and I
> trust it may survive us all, untouched by the axe—the
> sacrilegious axe which I so much dread. I feel for the mutila-
> tion of a tree just as I do for that of a human being, and
> would rather see a tree cut down than have a branch
> lopped. Wonderful is the sagacity they show in putting a
> growth here and a growth there, to suit their situation [she
> was no doubt thinking of her Yew tree, which now makes
> three separate yews] and I love to see the way in which
> they root themselves in our stony ground. I could wish that
> all my grandchildren would find in natural objects the
> pleasure they have given me.
> [It has come true in the case of most of her eight grand-
> daughters and six grandsons, not forgetting the great-
> grandsons.]
> I have felt an exaltation of happiness. Many a sunset has
> sent a glow to my heart, and I should think there is no one
> who has not felt awed by a clear starlight night, or has failed
> to respond to the beauty of moonlight.
> I remember once, in a time of great anxiety and trouble,
> that a harebell on the roadside was a real comfort to me
> with its purity and grace.

So Nain's early years had held things which kept her gay, at
times, to the end.

Not that, as a Grown-Up, she was to know an untroubled
life.

Far from it.

Shattering disillusionments of which she never spoke, were
to come. Financial losses, which would have shaken and
soured some natures...

Serenely Nain rode the storm-waves, as she had in earlier

days ridden her *ceffyl aur,* golden (i.e. bay) horse over her loved hills of Merioneth.

Cruel bereavements were behind her and ahead. The untimely passing of an idolised daughter resulted later in long physical pain for herself. She was not to be crushed. It was then, I suppose, that the comfort and beauty of Nature, even of that wayside harebell 'in its purity and grace' could help.

She could put aside mourning for what *had been* and prize what she still *had.* Her beloved daughter's child Bernard Darwin she cherished as Chief Grandson. He notes in his memoirs how Nain entered into and applauded every interest, every activity of his. I wonder the rest of his cousins didn't hate and resent that boy. We didn't. Even though in the eyes of his own and some of our Grown-Ups he could do no wrong. Even when he *had.* It made no difference.

Flash-back to that time at Aberdovey. We met for Christmas midday dinner in Nain's winter-lodgings at the tall big-roomed house Otago. (It is still so called, though it is now split up into modern egg-box flats.) 'We' means Bernard, with silky straight fringe in a Pre-Beatle hair-do, wearing a Pre-Etonian, snowy Eton collar; Bernard's father (bearded Uncle Frank Darwin the botanist); his old school friend, my father, whom he called 'Atty' for Arthur; myself in a spotless white feeder tied over my best green Nain-smocked short frock and put to sit on a cushion on the horse-hair sofa next to my cousin, two years older, what an honour! and I forget who else.

I remember the heavenly smell of turkey by Mary Morris, a superb cook. Her daughter Sara Morris, who refused to wear a cap, waited at table.

Nain, as ever, had carved the turkey, and expertly! as she sat.

'I hope none of my descendants *disgrace* me,' she said, severely—in fun, 'by *standing up* to carve.'

Bernard laughed aloud!

He probably knew (having *'the gipsy eyes that see but never*

weep') that all the other Grown-Ups were guilty of this
degenerate habit? Laughing, he leant forward to look at his
father, opposite, putting his elbow on the table and—Over
went his plate! spilling its lavish load in an avalanche of roast
turkey, stuffing, sausages, creamy mashed potato, tender
sprouts and rich gravy.

Swiftly Bernard turned on me—*Me,* harmless little cousin
sitting there as good as gold not saying a word, what had *I*
done? Nothing at all, not even joggled his elbow . . . Often,
since, I've wondered *why* this involuntary quick reaction and
found no answer . . . He dealt me a swift slap.

Nobody knew what to say. So nobody said anything . . .
Except Nain, serenely, to Sara Morris,

'Fetch another plate for Master Bernard.'

IV

Years before that, Nain had had fun in London. On visits to
well-off friends she had met famous stage-folk (*beautiful Mary
Anderson . . . dear Miss Ellen Terry*).

Nain, too, had talked with authors of note: Mark Twain,
Mary Anne Evans (George Eliot) and Bret Harte. This was
long after he had left the Wild West described in his short
stories *The Outcasts of Poker Flat* and *Tennessee's Partner.*

'How can you write so vividly about places and things you
haven't been near for such a long time?'

He made Nain a little bow and said simply,

'I can *remember.* All. As if it were yesterday.'

Today Sir Compton Mackenzie can lay claims to retaining
that gift.

Nain had enjoyed, in London, a further privilege.

She had actually heard and seen Charles Dickens in the flesh
at whatever packed Hall it was—possibly The Aquarium?—
where he was giving one of his readings-aloud from his novels.
Could he have given these more dramatically than they were
done in recent years by that most perfect interpreter, the gifted
stage-artist and playwright, our countryman, Emlyn Williams?
He, too, '*alone on the stage, holds an audience enthralled for*

G

two hours.' This was reported to me, from Canada.

Nain, as a young married woman, took with her to this 'personal appearance' of Dickens her two elder little boys, Arthur and Dickie.

'So she did,' said Father when I questioned him greedily for details of this epic treat. 'By Jove! I'd forgotten all about it.'

I swallowed my feelings. At least he could tell me if it had been the reading version of that hungry little workhouse waif asking for more? It couldn't have been the terrifying death of Bill Sikes from the house-tops . . . ?

'Surely you remember *something,* Father?'

'Some ladies fainted. . . . And—I remember your Uncle Dickie and I were given buns.'

Buns! And *fainting ladies.* . . . Were these the only memories of a unique literary event that they had brought back?

Soulless, exasperating little boys! I'm glad I didn't know them at that phase.

V

After her highly-stimulating days of gadding about London and of contacting interesting personalities of the times, behold Nain, settled down to being Buried Alive (as many would see it) in the quietest of Welsh valleys.

No swift car-transport to whisk one away-from-it-all as often as one wished, in those days! Nain stayed put at her old home Pantlludw. She always pronounced this word as if it were the Christian name of a favoured lover.

No meetings with the intriguing famous! Nain had many neighbouring family-friends with whom to sit gossiping over local affairs. 'Squeaks from the Parish pump' as these have been called; I mention no names. Outrageously rude were *some* of her young male descendants on the subject of Nain's Old Friends! She refused to find them boring. She, I suppose, could strike sparks out of anybody she entertained, could make *them* entertaining—to her.

No more mountain-rides and rambles as years went on; but

she cultivated her garden, her dear lily-garden with its thick
border of low-growing sedum, its pink blossom almost hidden
by wings of alighted feasting Red Admirals. (Sight, now, a
thing of the Past.) In the kitchen garden she had her great
hedge of sweet-peas, the small-flowered, sweet-peas of stronger
scent than those bred-for-size-and-colour modern seed-
catalogue varieties. Wonderful strawberries—Well, my grandfather had been responsible for those, but it remained Nain's
proud delight to lavish them on all visitors, even on all greedy
grandchildren.

On the wettest days she could sit by herself on the wooden
rustic bench of Pantlludw veranda. Over her head on the wall
hung the old dinner-gong (its vibrations could be heard from
up in the croquet-ground, down in the lily garden). At her
feet spread the slate slabs on one of which was carved the out-
line of the 20 lb. salmon caught in the Dovey by her son Arthur.
With that great tent of the ancient Yew-tree to the left of her,
the tree-crowded slope and its rare tulip tree to the right of her,
Nain would sit listening contentedly to what she called 'the
pleasant, continuous patter of the rain on the leaves!'

VI

She had another way of gathering the honey of fun from the
weed of Nothing Happening. She was a *collector*.

There are many sorts. Some collect stamps, prizing the
macabre rarity of those picked up in the sea after a wrecked air-
mail. Others go for first editions. Nain collected 'Come-from'.

Like so many of the Welsh, she'd a passion for genealogy.
Pedigrees. Family records. She adored delving into the past—
not only of her own family! Writing for their origins. Sometimes she'd even excavated pieces of bygone history which
the current descendants might have preferred to have left in
limbo . . . Nain had no opinion of The Jumped-Up who
ignored the jump—'pretentious' she (privately) called them.

Her own pedigree was framed between two pieces of glass
to keep it from dropping to pieces. I don't think she was any
more interested in it than in those of other people, though I

have heard her lament, *'Oh, I shall die and then none of you will know who you ARE!'* (as if we were Pretendents to a reigning house) and *'Do not forget that you have the blood of Welsh princes in your veins!'*

'Well, who hasn't?' as I heard an Uncle murmur cynically. 'I expect most of those Princes lived in caves in the mountains, coming out to harry the English. . . .'

(Nain wasn't meant to hear this.)

She became a walking *Who's Who*. Of this valley she knew who'd married whom. Where they'd lived before. And before *that*. Which of them had emigrated in the surge to Patagonia where a big settlement of the Welsh still speak *only* their native tongue and Spanish. Nain knew how many collaterals of them had been The Grown-ups of local families still flourishing here.

She was delighted if she could come across any anecdotes which showed their characters or potentialities.

A bygone Ruck, on her husband's side and possibly spelled Rooke at that date? had signed his name in some book or on some page, where the signature is as black and clear today as it was in the Seventeenth Century when he wrote it—'Think of that!'

Nain declared the writer might have started a thriving business on the family-secret-writing-ink that remained for centuries indelibly clear black, and he might have made a great deal of money!

Nain was careless about money. Her attention being held, in a grip too firm by *'the things that are more excellent.'* No doubt she got more fun out of having unearthed this ink-mystery than out of the fortune (should it have made one.)

Countless correspondents shared her vivid interest. Fellow 'diggers' she had never seen, never would see! Nain, having acquired, kept them as life-long pen-friends. Believe it or not, I have as a leggy child often been sent ('Run, dear!') with a sheaf of ten, twelve plump envelopes addressed in Nain's clear pointed handwriting to congenial strangers, down Pantlludw's long umbrageous ferny drive to the scarlet letter-box, set in one of the stone pillars of Pantlludw gate and embossed with the capital letters E.R. for Edward VII.

They are still there, relics of a reign when people still *actually* enjoyed writing letters. Nain got enormous fun out of it. In any case she would have considered it Bad Manners (a crime!) not to answer every letter by return of post . . . How she would have loathed the two-tiered system!

From his Mother our Father derived the criterion of what handwriting ought to be.

You should be able to pick any letter out of any word and to know at once, without any idea of the context, which letter of the alphabet it was. It's HAD it, that standard.

What ousted it?

The fact that you *do best* what you *enjoy* doing.

The Human Race, as Primitive Man a stage or so beyond the Naked Ape, knew the *Urge to Draw* ages before it discovered *Writing*.

Children kept the trace of that first Urge even to my day. Schools did *not* go for it. The Aim of the Education was to teach the child to *write,* and a good copybook hand at that. Copperplate was in.

Out, now!

Over-worked teachers of an over-large class of small pupils have found it a sound plan to give out as an exercise.

Try to draw something you saw on the way here.

The whole class is keen to Grab Chalks and At it. So, in place of a task that bores the kids a good time is had by all. In fact, Fun.

Today's grandchildren and great-grandchildren can, most of them, *draw and paint.* So did we. But less well, face it! than today's Katies, Glyns, Anthonys. Many of their productions are outstanding. I don't mean those framed efforts in carefully arranged Exhibitions of Children's Art in London galleries, but their home-done 'scribbles' as some Grown-Ups might call them. Pages, torn from a Primary School exercise-book, and carelessly dropped under the kitchen table, are covered with recognisable shapes of cars. A jet aircraft. A boy tramping home through the snow with—here's an 'observed' touch!—a trail of his foot-prints behind him. All as simple, live, real, and right, as in prehistoric cave-drawings by artists who *looked* at the beasts that they hunted.

Children turn with glee to plasticine ('Oh, the mess!') for modelling. I watched a young mother making pastry. Her little girl pinched bits of the dough. In no time a faceless but human shape—head, torso, limbs—was laid on the pastry-board for our approval.

'If that were sent to an Exhibition of modern sculpture as *Recumbent figure* by some famous Grown-up Name,' I said, 'how solemnly it would be admired!' (This was before the gate-crash into the Royal Academy of a work not known to be by a child.)

And the colour-sense of these sub-Tens? Pinned up on a cupboard door you'll see a sheet of patterns in silhouetted poster-paint or of cut-outs of paper in colour all clashing, flashing, and fearlessly dashing as a bed of petunias . . . The Grown-Ups are going to have a Merry Christmas Card that will be, honestly, a work of Art. I have ceased to feel smugly shocked because this seven-year-old artist writes so much worse than I would have been allowed to do when I was there. (My mother had also kept the very much more rudimentary drawings of mine done on the backs of envelopes and dated: 'her $2\frac{1}{2}$ year'.)

Apparently you can't exercise both faculties in equal parts?

Even typewritten, formal business letters, that must be signed by hand, show a hieroglyphic in place of a signature. A typed elucidation stands beside it.

A lad who wrote to thank for some present an elderly short-sighted relative (not me!) jovially ended the customary scrawl:

> *Hope you can read this, if not, try playing it on the piano!*
>
> *Love*
> SCRIBBLE WIGGLE

Imagine Nain had she been confronted by this Modern Instance. I can see the Look lifted from her beautiful embroidery (a silken square on which she drew her own design, with her needle, from the living flower). I can hear her gently-voiced but withering : 'FIE !'

It was only the lad's little joke ?

But Nain would not have thought it funny. Or fun.

Chapter Twelve
Bird on the Sill

I

It happens quite often on this coastal stretch of Wales.

Early one morning you go to your window. You look out to see if that thick quilt of grey cloud is the sky that means a whole dull day, or the *Rain before seven, clear at eleven* kind —And there! unannounced! is the visitor; a bird on the sill.

Not the pert robin in the puffed red waistcoat who cocks his head with a side glance, then, on legs that seem so misleadingly slim for his rounded weight, hops in to peck up the crumbs he knew would be there.

This is a homing pigeon on its return journey.

Some of them are travel-worn; and tatty as an old shuttle-cock.

But the last refugee we had here was in beautiful condition. Smooth glossy plumage of white, patterned with piebald flecks of russet and brown. Plumply busted as the Principal Boy of old time pantomime. Pink leg braceletted by the small shiny metal clip with its Club number.

Has it been blown off its course? Is it fatigue? Velocity not up to a long-distance flight? We, with whom it has taken refuge, do not know from what distance it has been loosed before it makes for the nearest landing-place. It is obviously used to human beings, trusts them. Its first and urgent need is

water. Drinking water comes before feeding it. Then rest, for
how long only the bird knows. Two, three days? It's welcomed. Then it's gone.

My sister had one harbouring in a garden-shed for a week.
Then, it flew on. Towards the Midlands? or perhaps further
north? but Merioneth is the more direct air-route for the
Midlands.

I was told this by a Midlander, with other details from
other (human) visitors to these parts.

II

During the summer holiday season, you cannot sit down on a
bench on the 'Prom' to watch the yachts butterflying across
the Estuary, the Sea-School lads handling their canoes, before
other watchers start friendly conversation. Asking if you live
here? Volunteering that they have driven down, are in rooms,
or at The Dovey here, and generally! that they come from the
Midlands. If you wish conversation fluently to continue, say
you have heard that in the Midlands there is a good deal of
pigeon-fancying?

'Ah! There is that!'

You will be told of a Pigeon-flying Club. People join and put
£1 into the Pool. A record is kept of the number of each bird.
—It's on a small clip fastened to its leg . . . 'You've seen that?
A good bird costs anything from twenty to thirty pounds. Did
you know that? Three years it takes to train them . . . Why,
of course, the birds all know their owners, absolutely! Same
as a dog does. He'll *talk* to his bird, quite naturally, like a man
to his dog.'

A Midlands wife told me about feeding them. 'They drink
enormously! . . . A pigeon-owner has to have great bowls of
fresh water laid down all the time for them. *And* they're so
fond of green stuff. You'll see them take up a scrap of lettuce-
heart like this—' Her small, sunburnt hand imitated it, 'and
pick at it, so delicately.'

'Competing birds,' said the man, 'are taken out in great
crates to the start . . . Might be France. Or Spain. Then loosed

. . . Marvellous how all know their way home. Some fly right back, straight as a die. First bird home wins the big money prize off the Pool. . . . There's also a second and third . . . Depends upon the Club, of course . . . Well, the birds are loosed —and you can't do any more about it . . . Fog! That seems to upset their—Whatever's their radar . . . Rain doesn't matter. Fog baffles them. Fog gets birds *down*.'

'Gets us all down.'

'*Winds* are the enemy too. The big risk. Who's to know when a sudden wind may get up, and where from, in which direction, and which of all these pigeons will be so placed that it sails along with it, the wind, while another one gets blown clean off course?'

I saw again that glossy shapely bird at rest on our sill. Who, indeed, could tell what fog over the sea might have blurred its radar instinct? Against what blasts of wind it had fought to make for the nearest land and the first human habitation? Human beings, it knew from experience, were *kind*. (It had no knowledge of others!) Man could be trusted to give it drink, food, and a static perching-place until, rested, it could take off for the last lap to home and haven with its known master.

'. . . If a pigeon is missing for more than a couple of days it is advertised and the number taken.'

I'd heard this from a friend on whose sill *two* pigeons had sought refuge. The birds appeared to feel that they had found a home from home. (Certain human beings show this trait. They are Never-Goers.) The hosts became bored. They decided to cease feeding these uninvited guests, who now, surely, would fly on, hungry? No. They descended to the garden and raided the young cabbages.

At last one flew on. The other continued to outstay his welcome.

The hosts approached (via its number and the Club) the bird's owner.

The answer came back with acknowledgements and careful instructions as to address and packing in a wooden box with plenty of air-holes in the lid. A postscript was added in

another, a careful, capital-lettered, little-boy-writing.—
YOU MAY KEEP HIM IF YOU LIKE (!)
  Sad to think that a child can grow tired of a pet. Or was it
—Let's hope it was a sympathetic generous impulse!

  'Ah, it's all a gamble, *what'll* happen in this game,' said the
Midlander on a note of heart-felt satisfaction. 'Just a big
gamble!'
  I remembered one of Nain's many collected gipsy sayings.
'Never despair of your LUCK! It takes but a moment to bring
it.'
  I remembered Harold Nicolson's admission, 'I am always
fascinated by the part played in human destinies by the ele-
ment of chance.'
  The Mystery of Chance, of whether or no the next moment
will bring Luck, is more than the money involved. The dear
gamble! How close it sticks to the heart of Everyman!

III

Another point about the visit of the racing-pigeon. It has the
Charm of the Impermanent: the poet's *'joy as it flies.'* Blake
knew it. Don't try to keep it, for it will not, cannot stay.
  Beginner's Luck at games or sport can be as a bird on the
sill. Your effortless catch that saved the match for your school.
You've never repeated that. You never even turned out as
much of a cricketer. Still, you've never got over the proud
thrill of that long ago achievement, even now that you're
middle-aged and sit watching cricket at Lord's, with your
grandson. He's the age you were that time when—'Ah, if I'd
kept that up . . . Be as good as any of these young chaps.'
  Holiday friendships are made on the sun-baked foreign
beach, the leisured cruise. People feel congenial from the word
Go. They are inseparables for the whole trip. Parting is a
wrench. (*But we'll meet in London.*) They exchange addresses,
telephone-numbers, promises to ring up, write, make a date . . .
  They don't.

Some distant day one or other of them will turn out a desk drawer, find an old snapshot. 'Now who on earth was THAT?'

First Love in its various transient forms, with all its ecstasy, its agony. . . . I've heard a young voice, not long broken into its manhood, say with unexpected philosophy this true thing: 'Well, that was that . . . I have had this. . . . I shall fall in love again. I may be hurt again. Get over it. I expect I shall marry. But *I have been through this*. It will not come back. Not the same. Not this.'

IV

Once on a train-journey I gleaned something of another aspect.

It was in the dear days when you could get in at Paddington and would be taken in comfort to your journey's end.

There was only one other passenger in the carriage. Sitting in the corner seat opposite to mine. Reading *The Daily Sketch*. I was immersed in the last exciting adventure of Lord Peter Wimsey and did not hear a rustle when sandwiches were taken out. She ate, tidily. She put the folded sandwich paper into the ash-tray. At Shrewsbury she looked out, beckoned to the boy who had wheeled up the tea-trolley and took coffee. Carefully she put the cup under the seat. Then she took out her knitting. Pale-blue. It would be. She was a fading blonde. And, like the character in John Betjeman's tea-shop poem, she was '*Such a very ordinary little woman*'. She counted stitches. Silently. She hadn't uttered a word, except to the trolley-boy, since we left Paddington; good! I was held by the witty remarks of Lord Peter Wimsey . . . until I sensed that reminding nudge to the mind that comes when you're nearing the Border. You look out; small cattle in the fields are all black. You look up; the view is of hills . . . ah, home.

My fellow-traveller stopped knitting and looked out too. Surprisingly: for I had seen she was not Welsh. She caught my eyes and said one word.

'Wales.'

'Yes. Are you going to Aberdovey?'

'No. Aberystwyth.'

'Oh. Then you will have to change at—'

'I know, I know. I've been. Often.'

She took her work up from her lap and it seemed she would speak no more.

However, further down the line—we'd left Llanbrynmair— she told me :

'I have to go a little way *out* of Aberystwyth. They'll meet me. It's a farm.'

If she had been Welsh she would already have told me the name of the farm, and of the family who owned it. Of where it was, exactly; and much of their family-history . . . She counted more stitches, began another row. Finally she volunteered :

'I am going to stay with my husband's people.'

She sounded as if she were really glad, fond of her in-laws. So we'd that in common. I forsook Lord Peter, and looked across at her in a tell-me-about-them way. She'd turned to look down at a drop below the railway bank. Ferns, the bright green ferns that spread themselves all over Wales, veiled the course of a hurrying little mountain stream.

She turned back and said,

'It's nice at the farm.' She spoke as if measuring milk, slowly. 'I go to them every summer. About this time. Just for a short visit. Every summer I go.'

I'd thought she was a widow. I nodded.

Presently she said what I hadn't thought.

'They are my *first* husband's people.'

'Oh ?'

'Yes. The other one's dead now, too. My *first* husband— killed in the War; we were only married six months—would have had the farm. . . . I go there every summer, just for a little visit . . . *Twenty-seven, twenty-eight*—' She was busily counting stitches half-aloud now. Obviously did not want to talk.

Familiar stretches of the countryside fled past between the well-known station-names. I sat, wondering what her story was . . . or if she had a story ?

At the Junction she got out quickly. I handed down to her a parcel she would have left behind on the rack.

—'Oh, dear! The *toys*! . . . my little nephews . . . !' She smiled her 'thank you', and I saw she had been pretty. Then she said, as a goodbye, or because it was something she must, MUST say aloud to somebody? the few words that told me her story.

'You never quite forget a Welshman, can you?'

For her the bird on the sill had left a soft feather of remembrance.

Chapter Thirteen
Legacies not in the Will

I

Are you among those who are thrilled by newspaper announcements of How Much people (perfectly strange names to you)
have left to their heirs? Do you scan all paragraphs headed
RECENT WILLS?

Yet the interesting legacies are those which are not mentioned.

More important than landed property, worth more than
'gold, or coin of silver shine', is the inheritance of sound
healthy constitution.

More betraying of origin than any genealogical table are
looks, tastes, tricks of speech or manner. Children who never
set eyes on their long-dead or distant relatives will show a
startling facial likeness, a gesture . . .

Lorna Wood, in her poem *To a Descendant,* promises 'not
to materialise' as the type of ghost who jangles chains, causes
draughts, carries her head ('a useless kind of chore'), spoils
the 'let' and has to be exorcised by the Rector—

> '*But I shall be pleased if anyone ever sees me*
> *In the sudden turn of your head or your laughing eyes.*'

Certain types of Nationals hark back to ancestors not of their own country. You see Irish people with all the dark handsomeness of Spaniards. There were wrecks from the Armada on the shores of their Island.

Some of the Welsh veer away from the short, compact, wiry Iberian or Celtic types. They produce offspring taller, more regular-featured, soldierly. Throw-backs to four hundred years of Roman Occupation of Ancient Britain.

Haven't you noticed a policeman patrolling the single street of a Welsh village, and seen how his helmet needs only a slight re-shaping to turn his head into that of one of Caesar's Legionaries? . . . One of those Roman soldiers, wounded and lying slumped in the heather, is approached, timidly, compassionately, by a peasant-maiden of the invaded territory . . . (Yes, I know. That's one of the 'squarer' pictures in the Tate Gallery. But a likely story seems to have occurred to the artist.) Haven't you found yourself handing your fare to the driver of a bus along a mountain-road who might, from his profile, have had a forebear who marched with those legions? Might even have helped to lay that road? Blood will tell.

Or do you consider that *Environment* is an influence more potent than *Heredity*?

Environment has quite a say.

What about the children who have never known their parentage, and have grown up showing all the characteristics of the cherishing foster-family?

What about German and Italian prisoners-of-war, who, finding the British way of life (in peace-time) sympathetic, had married and settled down here? Some of them learned to speak Welsh quite well. Their children, over the years, will scarcely be differentiated from their school-fellows.

Often, in a large family of brothers and sisters one or two—though of the same blood!—will stand out as different. Misfits. Rebels against the acceptances of their kin. Non-conformists against family-traditions. Why? *Circumstances* have led them into a way of life, a profession or job unfamiliar to the home-circle. Travel, sojourn in other countries could have revolutionised their outlook.—Friends, that would otherwise never have been met, can have had a vastly stronger impact than have any of those of his own blood upon the individual's whole being.

These factors are Legacies from Fate.

Would it be a good thing or not if we could screen, select, pick out *for ourselves* the inheritance that we preferred?

II

Fame, even fortune, I think, went to waste in a gift our Mother possessed and did not hand down to us.

Mother could come back from a party, a family-gathering, or merely an afternoon's shopping and could 'give' in mimicry any of the people she'd met. Not only their voices, what they'd said, but their whole personality would be reproduced. With fleeting gestures and facial expressions, and without words, she could convey the very clothes they wore. The people about them. Even their surroundings. . . . Cluttered Victorian drawing-room, Welsh village Post-office, chemist's-shop, rose before us.

Were you lucky enough to see Ruth Draper's one-woman shows? Alone on a London stage, she could turn it into the interior of an Italian Cathedral thronged by its shifting visitors —American tourists, humble devout worshippers, a woman having a rendezvous with her lover. Joyce Grenfell now has that hypnotic power. So had Mother. There was a streak of cruelty in it. As there has to be in any first-rate political cartoon by, say, Giles. When she did a running commentary it was with the caricaturist's necessary over-statement. Nobody could BE as surprised, pleased, agitated as Mother SEEMED when she put over Surprise, pleasure—or wrath. Where others might say: *'How those people irritated me,'* Mother's version was: *'Oh, how I LONGED to fell them to the EARTH!'*

Untaught star-quality Art! I believe it would have capti-

H

vated a sophisticated London audience—but for one thing.

She COULD not display it in public. Her 'house' was composed of her husband (Father, affecting to dismiss mimicry as a Monkey-Art hid behind his short dark moustache his enjoyment of it) and her children.

'Mother! "Do" So-and-so—'

She never refused us.

But raise her voice in any form of public speaking? Wild horses could not have dragged her on to a platform. She was reluctant to utter, even at the smallest, friendliest local Committee-meeting in session over some Good Cause.

'Will you second that, Mrs. Ruck?'

Mrs. Ruck could just lift a trembling hand.

She would return home exhausted.

Revived by a cup of tea and our audience-reaction she would exclaim: 'My Dears! I was TERRIFIED that they were going to ask me to answer questions!'

It happened: once.

At a meeting of St. Mark's the local Home for Waifs and Strays, it was suggested that visitors might act as 'godmothers' to such little girls as were without any relatives or friends who would write letters to, or take an interest in them.

Volunteer 'Godmothers' were found for all—except one. The Matron asked:

'Won't anybody have Dilys Morgan?' (not her real name).

Our Mother's, 'I will!' came in the damped-down squeak known in the family as The-Mouse-in-a-Bottle.

'Nobody?' queried Matron.

The lady sitting next to Mother spoke up.

'Mrs. Ruck says *she* will!'

Delightful, godmotherly letters were received by Dilys Morgan as long as Mother could take pen in hand.

Her children had all witnessed Mother's live renditions; none of 'the grandies' had.

Yet it was from a grandson who had only known her when he was a young schoolboy that I got one flash-back of her. He was describing a crashing bore among his associates.

'Soon as he appears the others make a bee-line for OUT—'

*Suddenly! There rose before me a cluster of backs in Air
Force blue disappearing, one by one. I had been made to see
them!*

—'There he sits. Left . . .'

*I saw the unfortunate man's glance round the deserted
Mess-room, the ash-trays with cigarettes thrown in half-
finished. He droops into a solitary armchair.*

'Pathetic, how grateful the chap is if anyone comes in and
speaks—'

*Lift of the head: I saw! . . . The Change into smiles. Arm-
chair dragged up close.*

'He's off! Braced to have anyone listen to weather-shop.'

And by gestures, intonations, Mother's grandson sketched
the Weather-man rise to his feet, stride to the opposite wall,
put up both arms to the framed chart, detach it from its hooks,
bring it across, and place it flat on the table before his listener,
held there in the attitude of the Wedding Guest, delayed by
the Ancient Mariner.

Here ended the rendition. Manlike, my son refuses to
remember the incident!

III

Gipsy-ancestry leaves its trace on the Welsh side of us.

The Romany Chal who moved in from Llanbrynmair with
a sack of gold thrown over his donkey's back may or may not
be a semi-fictitious character. But there is no denying the
physical legacies of that blood. Mrs. Lovell, a Caernarvon
gipsy, paid us regular visits in quest of tobacco for her short
clay pipe, and exclaimed each time she saw Father,

'God, he is like my Dolf!' (Adolphus Lovell was to the end
of his days a noted poacher.)

Typical gipsy Wanderlust was an addiction with our sister
Ursula. It drew her like a cord. Three times round the world
she'd gone, working her way in any job—companioning a
madly eccentric Hungarian lady on her wanderings, taking
sole charge of a baby-boy on the voyage from India—rather
than stay put for any time in the same place. Town-life would

have been impossible for her. She was happy when she joined a friend in a car-pilgrimage over the States, taking meals in the open. 'Never sleeping under a roof!' as she once wrote to Mother, adding that she had climbed a tree to stow their pot of honey on a branch so high that *bears* would not get at it in the night. . . .

A gipsy encampment, pitch for these nomads until quite lately, was the enthralling focus to us children, on our walks along the Towyn road. Vans, red and yellow; bonfires; busy enchanting people moving about!—We could watch through yawning gaps in the stonefence . . .

Modernity, foe to the genuinely traditional, has done away with it. No doubt the clear wide car-park is necessary. Order reigns instead of the higgledy-piggledy brambles and stones, puddles and mud that rose, sometimes up to the axles of the caravan wheels. No doubt these were not the 'better *class*' gipsies. These never cleaned camps. *Ach y fi!* (as the village complained). Old boots left to rot in the water! Nasty old sospans with the bottom out rusting in the grass! Filthy dirty old rags left hanging on the blackberry bushes! All gone now. Better so. But the gipsies—where? Even those 'better class' who burn their litter, keep their vans and camps cleaner than many a worthy citizen's back-kitchen, do not steal any washing they see on a line where they are. The well-known romantic-novelist-cum-efficient-philanthropist, Barbara Cartland, is the founder of a decent gipsy living-space. Barbara and her friends (good luck to them!) are fighting the legislation that sues the gipsy for remaining in one place long enough to enable him to send his children to school there. Then sues him because the children are not attending any school. . . . Such is the law.

'The Law,' as H. G. Wells wrote, 'is a mad Nurse put in charge of a restless child.'

Well, gipsy blood, even where there's only a trickle of it, is a very potent and durable strain.

For two generations now gipsy eyes, inherited from Amy *née* Ruck, have looked out of a Darwin face.

IV

One unlisted legacy was tossed carelessly down into our family by an extravagant forebear of our Mother's, one Lady Catherine West. She never asked the price of anything. She knew the Best. That quality was once prized as a status-symbol of discriminating Good Taste. In these days it becomes a handicap.

It has been inherited by a legatee together with a Welsh name from the other side of the family.

That by-gone Gwerfyl was a poet. *This* one is a conscientious young housewife. She goes forth to the shops with a list of Musts for her household and children. Thriftily she looks out for what comes well within her budget.

'*Ah, that*—' Before she can turn to the shop-assistant something happens. It's as if a hand points to another part of the shop—to another shop! It guides her, past what she had decided was Good Enough, to Something Better, to the Best.

Alas, the Best is the Most Expensive. The touch of a vanished hand, the slender white spectral hand that never touched a chore, does its stuff. The great-great-great-granddaughter of a woman whose criterion had been Quality would also have chosen before asking the price. Even when she hears the cost, she buys.

Afterwards she puts forward her only excuse. '*Lady Catherine went shopping!*'

V

Valuable bequests free of legacy-duty have been acknowledged in verse by the great German poet. From his father Goethe inherited his height, his *life's more earnest guidance,* and

Vom Mütterchen die Frohnatur und Lust zu fabuliren
(from Mother I've my gaiey and zest to tell a story!)

May I venture to say the same? That Old Scoundrel with the Hour-Glass has scythed away much of the unthinking gaiety. The zest in telling a story will, I trust, see me through.

Telling, my mind you. I like speaking better than writing. It's more my medium. Our Mother, who took away with her that gift of mimicry, left to each of her daughters something imponderable of her voice.

Remembered intonations of it—How often they are to be heard in the speech of one or other! Her sprinkling of a vocabulary, already lavish, with words used during her girlhood years passed abroad. ('I'll hastily *parcourir* this letter' . . . 'Sit down, child, don't *roder* about the room!') One of us at least has her narrative method beginning: 'I MUST tell you about—' some entirely ordinary even boring incident, and making it rise, with emphasis amounting purposefully to overstatement, through rivetting suspense, to melodramatic climax. All of us have inherited the clear diction for which I have received honourable mention from Luncheon Clubs and Women's Institutes.

It was left to me to make flagrant use, even bread-and-butter, at times! of Mother's speaking-voice.

Chapter Fourteen
Thanks from a
Serpent's Tooth

I

Father was a man who *fled* from babies.

He'd nothing to say, either, to toddlers who got in his way, who bumped down between his feet and set up a howl.

Until they were of a 'reasonable age' I verily believe he would have been content not to set eyes upon any of his eight children.

Mother explained it later: 'He just wasn't a "Cock-robin" Father'—

The Robin, you see, is one of the only two male birds who take turn with their wives to sit on the eggs in the nest. Sit, waiting patiently for the fledglings to be hatched out. The other bird is the Black-headed Warbler, who also sits, but to alleviate boredom, he sings. (Like a man in his bath.)

'Until they're bigger, their father's *hopeless*. Lots of men *are* like that.'

II

Fair play to the male parents of this day and age! One notices a distinct rise in the number of *un*reluctant (or cock-robin) fathers. Men, stalwart young he-men then can be seen all about the length and breadth of our coasts on holiday, gaily swinging the carri-cot by one handle while the Occupant's mother holds the other. Man after man-on-holiday strides beachwards with a toddler fearlessly astride his shoulders, balanced by holding on to his father's head. Often, a pram is wheeled unashamedly by Daddy; Mummy, carefree, cigarette in mouth, trips on frivolous Italian sandals alongside.

These sights, believe me! were not to be seen two generations back.

A man might be proud of, fond of his offspring. But—*A man did not wheel a pram.*

Would we, *as children,* have noticed whether they did or they didn't?

III

Automatically, children take an incredible number of things for granted. One was that there would always be Grown-ups to take care of them, if they needed taking care of . . . Another was that you never knew what the Grown-ups were going to do next. But—This was when you were still only knee-high to a Grown-up, there were plenty of things nearer the ground which were more interesting, other children, animals, shells, pebbles. *And,* in those far-distant pre-telly days, ah, *picture books . . . !*

There were three of us—Myself, a brother, a sister—when I first, vaguely, heard talk about 'A Great Change in our Lives' going on well over our heads. These heads were all dark, with silky straight hair done exactly as The Beatles were to do theirs more than half-a-century on. Vaguely I gleaned that perhaps Mother and Father were going out to India. They would leave us in Wales . . . In Aberdovey, that *exciting* place where we knew all those people. Nain, who'd given me that picture-book about *The Three Jovial Huntsmen, they hunted and they hollered, and Nothing did they find,* and that. . . . There would be John Bell—the life-boat. And the pier, with the sailing ships. The Bell children to play with, and Janesophia, the naughtiest little girl in the village, with whom we were fast friends. The old Blacksmith—

Aberdovey, I thought. Oh.

A long, *long* time seemed to go on. Nothing more happening about Change. Just life in Formby, Lancashire. I went to a little school and learnt about Joan of Arc. I went to Sunday School and listened to interesting stories told us by a man. I'd liked best the story he'd told us the Sunday before. He said,

'Little Amy is the youngest of you, and the only one who remembers what Jesus said to Jairus's daughter!' I'd told him my name was Amy. It *was* one of my names! and I liked it as a change.

That April we'd had the baby sister. White tulips on the font when she was christened. . . . Mary Ursula. Nothing happened.

Then, all at once! The Grown-ups were going to do something quite different.

We were all leaving Holly Cottage, Formby, Lancashire and going to *live* in Wales! Hurray! Not just for holidays and Father's leave. For good. In a town called Caernarvon, where there was an old Castle, like those in *Little Arthur's History of England*. Father, who used to be a soldier, was going to be a Policeman, sort of . . .

Not in Aberdovey. 'Oh!' I said.

Not India, either? No.

India, for me, had been the place where I was born, a bungalow called The Wren's Nest, close under the Himalayas. This I'd been told by Mother; I hadn't remembered it. India was my lovely and beloved chocolate-blancmange-coloured Ayah whom I just did remember. India, the jingling of those many slender silver bangles that Mother wore all the way up her forearm from her wrist to her elbow. Sometimes, when we lived at Fleetwood, she would strip them all off and toss them down on the carpet so that Baby Brother (O.L.R.) crawling on his hands and knees, would pick them up and hand them up to her one by one . . . India, the Hindustani words which still popped in and out of Mother's speech. Early tea was chota hasari. They called the garden the compound. Great butterflies flopped about flowers we'd never seen. People went about in 'rickshaws' drawn by 'natives'. Mother had loved her years in India. She'd said so. Often.

I asked Father—who by this time considered I was of a reasonable age and could communicate—I asked him :

'What would happen if we came out to India with Mother and you?'

'Several little Indian hillside graves, I expect,' said Father grimly.

At the time I hardly took in what this meant. In those days of no air-conditioning India was a dangerous climate for little English children.

Little we realised that for our sakes he had made a real sacrifice. Instead of joining his Regiment, as he would far have preferred to do, in an India which was still the British Raj, he put in for and was taken for the post of Chief Constable of Caernarvonshire (not yet Gwyneth and including Merioneth).

India, I thought, would have been nicer...

IV

Presently we found life in Caernarvonshire had become quite nice. Father was different. We elder ones had grown into creatures of an age in which he could take an interest...

They come back to me now... flash-backs of Summer evenings on the Menai Straits when two of us were actually lifted from the beds into which as Victorian children we'd been tucked in at half-past six. Wrapped in our winter overcoats over our nightgowns, and settled under rugs, we sat aboard the row-boat with Father and Mother. Slowly we drifted along the Caernarvonshire side. The Mountains of the Snowdon Range were darkening shapes against the clear sky. Echoes of the Grown-ups' talk.

'Look, children,' Mother's hand pointing. 'That's the Elephant Mountain. Isn't it exactly like an elephant's back?'

Father's deep-toned growl. . . . 'Those three-pointed peaks they call "The Rivals". They're not. The Welsh name is *Yr Eiffel* ... means a three-pronged fork.' ...

More talk about a climb he'd done up there . . . 'Wanted to have a look at an Iron-Age Fortress.'

Round, beautifully-constructed buildings they'd been. The Celts built them there because the richer Welsh valleys had been taken over and settled in by the Romans . . . When?

Echoes of dates for once noted by his eldest daughter and still remembered when almost every important date in English History has gone from her. . . . '400 B.C. to A.D. 500,' I heard . . . 'On that bare mountain-top. . . . Couldn't bring supplies up from Segontium (Caernarvon). The Celts went down the other slope, to Nevin. Four miles they'd leg it down there to get fish. They lived on shell-fish—'

'Yes!' Echo of Mother's quicker accents. 'You told me. Show the children what you found half buried up there, Arthur.'

Father shipped an oar, put a hand into a pocket. Held out on his big palm to the eyes of us small late-Victorians a cockle-shell, brittle white, left among the ruins of the 'Tre' r Ceiri' all that time ago.

It seems strange to me now, that meeting of the centuries. To me, then, it was just an ordinary Shell Father had picked up. We picked up much prettier fan shells and those break-able little pink oval ones we called 'sunset shells' off the beach at Aberdovey.

The last four of the eight of us were Caernarvonshire born. We took it for granted that Mother should be kept busy. She didn't seem to mind. Only years later I realised that she was the exact opposite of Father in (apparently) preferring the children to be very little. Almost sad because they had to grow up and would presently grow away.

V

It was Father who first took us—the now articulate 'us'—up stone steps into the over-grown courtyard of that celebrated Castle. It was not yet 'restored' or repaired. Suitable for an investiture of a Prince of Wales! Yellow wallflowers blazed out of every crevice, cranny, crack in the masonry. Father showed us which was Queen Eleanor's Gate. He took us up the spiralling stairs—'We're nearly there. Give me your hand, then,'—to the top of the Eagle Tower. We could look down over the Bridge across 'the Aber'. The hill of Coed Helen . . . a wood, called after the wife of a Roman Emperor when Caernarvon was Segontium.

I was glad to come down. Heights have always scared me (Except in an aeroplane, when one loses the sense of contact with the ground. Perhaps it's too far down to *matter*?)

Much happier I was when Father would have us brought, or we would find our way to his cramped little office in Castle Street. One wall of it was taken up by a big map of the county. Pins, stuck over rounds of pink confetti marked the where-abouts of the men known to us as 'Father's Policemen'.

'We're going *there* this afternoon,' he'd say, pointing with the stem of his pipe to some confetti-based pin.

One or more of us would be packed into the old pony-and-trap and away we'd go, clop, clop, out of town. Across the Bridge over the Seiont, past the park with the ponds where we fed ducks, past Bontnewydd, tiny village of all-stone cottages where a woman lived who made peppermint rock such as I've never tasted since ! Then past Dinas—

VI

This white house off the road and beyond the trees, belonged to Sir Owen Roberts the Welsh educationalist. There was a large garden, tennis-lawns, a long grass walk from the house to a flag-staff and a look-out over the sea. The family stayed there in the summer months. At once they had made friends with our parents. They gave big tennis-parties, followed by lavish tea in the garden. To these last we children, to our greedy delight, were included. The Owen-Roberts girls, Trixie and Lucy, seemed very grand and fashionable because, 'instead of having washing-day at home like everybody', they sent off parcels every week to a London laundry, with their frilly muslin frocks and lacy petticoats. The eldest daughter was called Margaret. Her I remember well with a straw-boater tilted to the front over her golden hair, a white blouse stiffly collared up to her chin and a long skirt down to her toes. In this outfit—Oh, visions of Wimbledon-to-come!—she played tennis with vigour and zest.

This Margaret was destined—little as anybody then dreamed of such a thing!—to become the grandmother of a front-page Celebrity who would ring the bells of London the wildest peal for years.

In our time she was newly-engaged to the clever young Harley Street specialist called Doctor Armstrong Jones. The white house Dinas with its long grass walk to the flag-staff and the sea-view was not yet *Plas* Dinas, to be visited by Royalty who had married the family's gifted grandson, Tony —now Lord Snowdon.

On, up, clop-clop, to some remote village and its mini-police station and the official inspection of 'Father's policemen'. A shirt-sleeved stalwart digging a potato patch. Thrusting spade into soil, he would stride forward. Slow converse would be carried on in Welsh . . .

Tea would be produced for all. Often, it was already on the table. Father would quote and translate for us a Welsh proverb: *'Never offer food and the food in the cupboard.'*

Home, then, sleepy and silent with enjoyment.

Did we thank Father for the treat? Taken for granted, I fear.

Later on drives by the old pony-and-cart were superseded by bicycle rides with Father to the remoter districts. Such as Beddgelert, where Father quoted the rhyme:

> *Under the shadow of Moel HeBog*
> *Is the grave of Llewelyn's remarkable dog.*

At another place—would it be Portmadoc? or Bettws-y-Coed?—the policeman was by way of what would now be called an Intellectual. He told Father he enjoyed reading *'Plat-*to' (sic.)

So often, Father, who had barred us as toddlers, took us with him! We expected it as a matter of course.

'A child's affection to its parent,' said E. Nesbit, 'is sixpence given in change for a sovereign.'

A sovereign, remember?—was the thick round piece of solid gold which stood for the pound, and which could, in those days, buy—Well, never mind that. Incidentally, at the Auction in aid of the Royal Welsh Agricultural Show, a sovereign, survival of other days! was put up as a single item. It fetched seven pounds . . .

When, as a Grown-up, I quoted her *mot* about sixpence to E. Nesbit, that writer of classic stories for and about children, she smiled,

'Did I say that? It's rather good, very sad, and quite true.'

'How sharper than a serpent's Tooth it is To have a thankless child.'

King Lear was not the only one. *Any*body, with *any* child, surely must have said, thought, felt it at one time or another?

Our Mother used, at some forgetfulness or carelessness to exclaim dramatically, 'Cruel, *cruel* children!'

Yet it was Father who, unbeknown to his casual youngsters, had given up most for them.

How?

Now, from the first, he and his policemen had got on. They liked and respected each other. In recent fan-letters to me there has been mention of the writer's father or grandfather who 'remembered your father in Caernarvon' . . . Often said, 'Colonel Ruck was something *like* a Chief *Constable* . . . an honourable gentleman!'

A Chief Constable who, years later, succeeded him showed me over the present Police Headquarters—How up-to-the-modern-minute, how palatially different from the little old Castle Street office!—This Chief Constable had been diverted from the fate of school-mastering by my cousin Dick Atkin, who had urged the parents—'Send that boy into the Police . . . He's made for that!'—This man, Colonel Williams, told me: 'You know, *my* ambition is to have things done in the way *your* father would have approved!'

If the job had involved only police work I think our Father would have been happy enough in it. There were times though when he loomed home like a thunder-cloud over Snowdon, tugging at his short dark moustache and muttering to Mother,

'*By* Jove! that County Council Committee Meeting— Business!'

It did not occur to any of us for years what it must often have meant to a man of his Old Army *genre* without a clue (or a care) how to avoid being unpopular, or of what might be the more tactful way. The word 'Expediency' had been left out of Father's vocabulary.

And out of Father.

Surely he would have been thankful to chuck a position that became at times such—well, so uncongenial. He stuck it for over twenty years for our sakes. Thankless little self-absorbed serpents' teeth that we were.

Brightest flash-back of my childhood memories of Father came before Caernarvonshire days . . . Back, back to when he was Adjutant of the Liverpool Volunteers living at Formby, and when for his winter leave we all migrated to Wales.

We had reached the first stage of our journey. Vivid flash-back of the All-Change-here at Lime Street Station, for the Old Cambrian Railway. . . .

But we were conditioned to these changes and long waits. Patient family group around our stack of luggage . . . Heavens! the arkish trunks and ponderous portmanteaux of the period! not to mention the hooded, heavy roomy four-wheeled pram which no man ever wheeled.

Surreptitiously I slipped away . . . Eeled my way through the crush of passengers and porters and made for the railway bookstall. I was at the age when (like other imaginative children of that pre-Telly Era) I lived in a story-book world, more real and heavens! how much more thrilling than the grown-up world around. I was bent on a look-see at the enticing display of books . . . Behind me, father loomed up. . . . Wild hope rose. Could he, unprompted, have *guessed* how I hungered and thirsted for something to read in the train? No. He was only getting the *Liverpool Echo* for himself. *No!* He *was* buying a book. The one with the picture on the cover of a beautiful girl with a fish's tail. He pushed it into my eager eight-year-old paws with a gentle growl, 'Here.'

Word that was to open for me that magic undersea world. Oyster-shells on her silvery tail. Long hair streaming through the water behind her. Hair that must be sacrificed to the cruel sea-witch, yes, and her tongue as well, in exchange for a pair of legs like a human being with which to win the love of a mortal.

Even if I owed him nothing else I shall always worship Father for giving me *The Little Mermaid* by Hans Christian Andersen.

'Oh—!' Lost, I was beginning to read where I stood, against the bookstall.

'By Jove, train's in. Hurry.'

Clutching the Book with both hands to my chest I pushed sideways, through the wall of obstructing legs and sharp-edged luggage, after Father, put my head back to look up at him.

I hope—I *think* he heard my gasp of : 'Thank you, oh, THANK YOU.'

Chapter Fifteen
B.B.C. Cymru

I

Can you recall hearing the wireless announcement 'This is London calling—'? Possibly not.

And that song of the period:

> *Do you ree-mem-ber*
> *How every night we tried to get*
> *2 L.O. on the crystal set?*

It doesn't wake any echo?

For me it does. I spoke on 2 L.O. That was in days of extreme Yore. Unborn Tomorrow and B.B.C. Wales. I had published my first novel. *His Official Fiancée* had had Beginner's Luck. People over fifty still, apparently, remember that mild, naïve romance. Some of them in their school-girlhood had read it surreptitiously, in bed. They kept it hidden under the mattress from their Grown-Ups. I wonder what on earth their Grown-ups would have thought, or, for that matter what these secret readers themselves think of some of Today's bestsellers?

To return to the Day before Yesterday's Radio.

Off I went to Savoy Hill, the then-Headquarters. I was curiously *un*-excited about having been invited to read a short talk on *Heroines in Fiction*. At the time I was more involved in writing another novel about them. Odd, how much more important it still felt to see one's name *in print*.

I don't remember what I put into my hand-written script. All I do vividly recall about that Savoy Hill occasion is that I dropped a memorable clanger.

Knowing that my family in distant Merioneth would be clamped to the earphones (!!) of the set that had not long been installed at Esgair, I, in my innocence, concluded my remarks with a cheerful,

'Goodbye, everybody,' adding a special 'Goodbye, *Mother!*'
Had I incurred wrath!

'Miss Ruck, Miss Ruck! didn't you know that it is strictly forbidden to address Private Individuals?'

Later, I heard that Another Private Individual, my youngest listener, Ursula Hope Luck, was at that moment appealing to the Grown-Ups,

'May I give Aunt Berta a bit of my butterscotch now?'

Did the tiny creature imagine she could pop it down the ear-phones?

That broadcast had not deserved butterscotch. It wasn't good.

II

For me as for everybody else the world had become so full of a number of things before Radio became the force for Entertainment, Communication, Politics, Education that it is now....

Still, years later, there was smouldering in me the ambition to get on 'the wireless' again.

I had listened to friends speaking. J. B. Priestley's forthright comments on War in our time. Pamela Frankau's unique contralto, recognisable in the middle of any talk she was giving.

Why couldn't *I* have a try? I didn't know how to set about it.

Chance helped.

By chance I met and made friends in a train with Cledwyn Hughes.

No! Not the M.P. That mistake is often made. This was Cledwyn who wrote *Royal Wales,* and who lives with his wife Lyn, the painter, at Arthog.

They were visited by Mr. Aled Vaughan, of the Welsh B.B.C., on business to do with Cledwyn's descriptions of the Welsh countryside in the varying seasons. Sensitive and beautifully written. Over the air they are read by someone else. Cledwyn himself admits, 'I am one of these *Mumblers.*' They'd arranged for a reader.

This Mr. Vaughan then asked if they could suggest anything else promising. They mentioned me and my Ladies' Luncheon Club and Adult Education for the Forces.

He said he'd look in on me at Aberdovey.

I blenched, for the first time. Still, it was what I *wanted*? We met...

I found this Mr. Vaughan quite unintimidating! A dark sensitive Celtic type with a W. B. Yeats lock of hair apt to fall over his brow. Quick-eyed! Curiously, for six months after his war-service in the R.A.F., this man had been *blind*. Could this, I was to wonder later, have brought home to him that loss of one sense can alert and sharpen other faculties? This is shown in his first novel *The Seduction,* published by Gollancz, and set in a centuries-old Welsh farm in modern times. The narrator has had his tongue brutally cut out in the war. Dumb, he hears, sees, apprehends with power beyond that of the other characters.

This immensely good, stark and haunting book had not been written at the time of my first meeting with its author. He made a date for me to broadcast on the Welsh B.B.C.

III

It was my first visit to Cardiff. About this place I'd known just two things. It had, my son the pilot had told me, the best airport in Britain. And one district of it possessed the sinister magical name of Tiger Bay.

In this most progressive, varied, international of cities I was to spend a night and a day and another night.

In a small intimate Spanish restaurant I lunched with Aled Vaughan, with Emyr Humphreys the distinguished Welsh novelist and contributor to the *Spectator,* and—I had not bargained for this—Mr. Kenneth Harris, then 'Pendennis' of the *Observer*'s Table-Talk, who was to be of the party.

Goodness, I thought, dismayed. One of these superior English Intellectuals going to put questions to me.

My mistake.

He was friendly and laughing. He'd a Welsh mother. I 'fell in like' with him at once.

Less and less can I understand why Caradoc Evans said, 'A happy Welshman is as rare as a bee in the snow—'

Lunch with these three typical ones was a light-hearted buzz. Discussion went on of questions to be put to me of my early life, school, start of work—any notabilities I'd met in long ago days. Days before any of these men were born!

Yet they made me feel quite happily back in those days and with them. Not every interviewer has this gift.

'—But don't, please, pour out any more of that potent red wine for me. I know I should begin to say indiscreet things.'

'Oh, do. That would be wonderful. *Be* indiscreet!'

'No.'

'Well!, we ought to be getting along to the studio. It'll be all right to be "live", Kenneth.' Mr. Vaughan turned to me. 'I'll want you to concentrate on those Edwardian parties.'

I often get Edwardian references to myself. My Edwardian accent. My Edwardian manner. Why? I lived through quite a stretch of Victoria first.

'Describe the different dress, the girls without make-up on; "one only saw face-coloured faces," as you said. *Concentrate* on that. Will you?'

'Yes. Oh, yes.' Concentrate on anything suggested; so pleased to consort with these new stimulating acquaintances who could strike sparks out of anyone, and to be all set for this new place, the goal of my ambition.

IV

So here we are, in Cardiff's Broadcasting House. Very different from that 2 L.O. place. Broadcasting studio in neutral colour like a salon for high-fashion. Sound-proof. Bare—but for the chairs, table, silent clock of which the hand moves not by the 'unforgiving minute' but by the second.

Production is rationed by the half, or is it the quarter-second?

Kenneth Harris, with note-book, sits down opposite me. Smiles encouragingly.

'It's only the run-over first.'

Aled Vaughan says,

'You won't be afraid of the mike?'

'Which *is* the mike?' It stands on the table. 'Oh, that.'

Aled disappears into an adjoining room to become a discarnate intelligence, a voice that directs, checks—'Go back to . . .'—encourages, says, 'Don't keep her too *factual,* Kenneth. I want plenty of—'

—of whatever Edwardian echoes I was sounding.

At the end of the afternoon he asks,

'You aren't *tired*? The incredible woman isn't tired, Kenneth!'

I say, 'It was *Fun*!'

Unfailing recipe for avoiding any looming threat of fatigue in work or play.

V

Even more fun were the next broadcastings. Six of them in a row, this time. It was in the studios in Swansea that I spent two concentrated days of working under Aled (now a valued friend), rehearsing, then recording. Three times a day—morning, afternoon, evening. This was for the series of Talks that came out on Sunday mornings weeks later under the covering title *A Smile for the Past.* Some of the material was published later in book form. Most of the incidents were Aled's preferences—Edwardian theatrical memories.

Stage star Ernest Thesiger, my fellow-student of Art School days, wrote,

'I heard you were mentioning Me and hoped that you were going to be libellous so that I might sue you for vast sums, but I was disappointed. You did me very well so I suppose I must be grateful.'

He'd always teased me a good deal: I was a black-haired Savage from the Wilds, and—'Oh, Ruckie, what a *Cat* you are!'

'Catty is a thing I never was. Not clever enough, Ernest.'

He, who could play anything from the Silly Ass who kept us in stitches at that farce *A Little Bit of Fluff* to the Polonius that was acclaimed to the echo in Russia, wrote, 'All publicity is caviar to an actor!' but thanked me for it, very gracefully.

Surprising was the number of other letters elicited by that series.

The first of all ever addressed to 'Berta Ruck B.B.C., LONDON' (a real thrill) came from Paris, and from someone of whom I was a fan. We'd met by correspondence only. Nancy Mitford had switched on casually. Approved the sound of a U-voice ('U' or 'non-U' was her own classification-phrase). Approved what I said about the boon of modern and universal make-up. I had said, 'No red-haired girl need suffer nowadays from having white eye-lashes.' And, at the announcer's final—'You have been listening to—' Miss Mitford had exclaimed aloud, 'Why! It was my pen-pal.'

A Yorkshire housewife actually stopped in the middle of baking a pie to listen to me.

An artist's model, now seventy, was 'reminded of happy days, sitting to Mr. Orpen and Mr. Augustus John.'

An old (Regular) Army Officer who remembered the Music-halls, the old Music-halls of which I spoke, addressed me as 'Lady' (quite Shakespearian) and sent best wishes that I might live long enough to make many more of these splendid broadcasts! And so on.

'How you can! . . . I,' declare certain friends, 'would die of nervousness.' Then, with almost morbid curiosity about these mysteries, 'What's is *like*? What do you *do*?'

Well! You go in. Radio-studios are much of a pattern. Producers are, in my experience, all sympathetic, young men-and-brothers. Moderns, with beautiful old names out of The Mabinogion—(adapted for *The Idylls of the King*) Gareth, Geraint, Dyfnallt. There's a well-known She-producer too; Teleri.

You sit down at the table. In front of you is that mike, that small lamp, and your script. This last has of course already been carefully vetted *and cut,* since, as I realised, every quarter-second is relentlessly rationed. The producer says, 'Give us a line, Berta, please.' You read the first dozen words of your script quite ordinarily, as if you were telling what it's about.

The producer says 'O.K.' Or it may be he turns and enquires as if into the void, 'How's that, Cardiff? . . . O.K.' Turning back to you he says, 'Now, watch for the green light. When the green light goes on, you start.'

You fix your eyes on the small lamp. Perhaps you count ten, like a parachutist at the jump. The green light goes on, bright as a madly enthusiastic glow-worm and it's the off.

You read your script in your ordinary voice as for the 'line'. You already know about being careful to put each page of your script, as you finish it, down to your right on the table and to avoid a rustle.

'Fine,' says the producer as you finish.

Alternatively, 'Sorry! It's still half-a-minute too long. Have to cut.'

So we discuss *where*.

And re-start.

'It all sounds *too* terrifying,' sigh lay-minded friends. 'You're used to talking to the W.I.; you say an audience helps? Doesn't it make it even Worse when you can't *see* any audience?'

'But you can! You can see the expression of your Producer. You've got whoever those lads are so busy behind the aquarium —I mean the glass-screen between the studio and the other room! You can *tell* when they are amused.'

'I should never have got beyond that GHASTLY moment when I was told to "watch the green light" !'

I haven't inherited my Mother's 'platform panic'.

I simply think: Well, I *can* only do what I *can*. I was put up here for that, so here goes.

À propos stage-fright, the French have a saying, *No good actor plays in a dry shirt*. Sweating with apprehension and 'foot-lights fever' he goes on. Dripping, he comes off. More especially on a first night.

Gifted stage-friends of mine—famous, acclaimed, experienced—have told me that they are like this. They may not— and do not—give a sign of it during their performance, but after years of success they remain like this.

If that French *mot* held good without exception I should be no earthly use for radio. Is it conceit to say I must have *some* entertainment-value? Otherwise, should I have been asked twice? Otherwise, should I have got fan-mail from strangers to say they listened to every word and it was exactly as if I was in the room! Even people who know me well say so. Even those who, if I *were* in the room, dishing out what I think is good advice or words of wisdom, would not take the slightest notice. Such is the prestige, the power of the radio-set.

The 'Oscar' in this kind was won after I had read over the air one of the eerie atmospheric ghost-stories of my husband, Oliver Onions, entitled *House Full*.

Ruthlessly I must here condense all but the salient points. Here's the gist:

The time: 1936. The place: a shabby come-down, family-hotel-cum-saloon-bar. A moody Mr. Somebody arrives in search of cheap lodgings where he can work quietly at a musical composition. . . . Included in the make-shift furniture of the Bar are two blocks of old theatre-stalls fastened together. Gilded, cushioned in red velvet, they keep the air of having known better days before they were knocked down for a song at some auction sale. The young composer stares at them, mutters: 'full of echoes'. He rents the upper room with a piano, where he can work. Presently,

oddly! he prefers to bring down his note-book and scribble
in a corner of the Bar. 'It's those chairs,' he explains, un-
intelligibly. Somehow they seem to help, to be a fluctuating
inspiration. . . . Presently, too, he becomes 'Harry' and is
like one of the family. He falls for Anne, daughter of the
house. On a winter's night she is helping him to turn out
the lights in the Bar. 'How's it going, your piece?' she asks
diffidently. 'Rottenly,' he mutters. For what is there to put
heart into an artist who is trying to do something a bit
different for a lot of clots who don't want that, only want
him to do what they want? . . . It is almost dark. Suddenly
a coal drops in the dying fire. It shoots up again in flame.
The whole place—or was it only those two rows of fauteuils,
is softly illuminated, and seen to be full of shimmering, bare-
shouldered ladies in satin and diamonds, their escorts in
white ties and tails who have brought them to this first
night of an Opera. Ghosts? But Harry sees them! . . . He
meets Anne's amazed eyes. . . . She, too? There is around
them a murmur of soft talk, a rustling of programmes, a
tuning-up of violins, a throb in the haunted air. Heavy
fringed curtains with the mellow glow of the footlights on
them part, the conductor's baton makes tut-tut, and out!
breaks the merry lilting music of which Harry knows every
note that is to come, for every note is his.

This letter came after the broadcast and from somewhere
in the North. It was headed by the modern-looking address
of an orchestra, possibly of a dance-band, and said:

It was a good story, but believe me, Madam, if you had
read aloud a page from a Railway Guide I should have
listened to you with equal delight, for I am a musician and
can follow the shades of the human voice.

How Mother would have preened over this tribute to *her*
way of speaking. Honour to whom honour is due. Good shot!
. . . Her bird!

VI

STORY-TELLER TO THE TROOPS

Someone had blundered. That, I'm afraid, was how I first found myself in that war-time job of giving talks to audiences of the Services.

Someone in search of speakers to the Troops had heard that there was now, staying in Aberdovey, a novelist, who 'spoke' to Ladies Luncheon-Clubs, and so on. Someone else put in that this writer was an Authority on Dickens.

This, as it turned out too late! meant that I had been confused with—of all people!—my first cousin Bernard Darwin, who wrote on Sport and also those memorable first leaders for *The Times*. These last nearly always brought in a quotation from Dickens.

Bernard knew him virtually by heart.

I could repeat a *certain* amount of that Master. Enough to argue, sometimes quite violently, with Bernard.

It was to me that they wrote . . . Officially!

Anyhow! That, briefly, was how it came to my finding myself put up on a platform in a half-lighted hall somewhere in South Wales, facing a row of half-seen girls in khaki uniform. There were quarter-seen rows of them behind these.

With the mateyness mingled with respect that came naturally, that autumn of 1940–41 between those who were serving their country in comfortless surroundings and those who had been sent if possible to entertain them, I began,

'Well, ladies and—a *few* gentlemen, for I see some of you have brought the boy-friend in here with you out of the wet'— and at once I got the feel of something I'd learnt about in peacetime Luncheon Clubs. Audience reaction. They were prepared to like me and whatever was my little turn. And thankful, no doubt, to hear anything that *wasn't* barked words of command and the sound of the rain on the roof?

Most of it impromptu and all of it without notes (which are hated by the Welsh, they like you to 'tell') I gave them a

précis of several pages of *David Copperfield*. Peggotty and his
boat. Little Em'ly. The Master's magic held. I suppose they
were too young, too modern, too radio-minded to have *read*
it? They listened.

I told them how my cousin (a *real* Dickens expert) and I
had wrangled over the character of David's hero, Steerforth.

Bernard Darwin had roundly declared that: 'David Copperfield (and even Dickens himself for that matter) never knew
what an absolute *cad* Steerforth was.'

'He *did* know, Bernard.' We had walked to the length and
back of a small country railway-station (Glandyfi junction, it
was) discussing this as earnestly as if it was a burning question
of the day. '*He knew.*'

'Couldn't have, or he wouldn't have gone about with him.'

'He *loved* him! He gave him a hero's death—' (we nar-
rowly missed the train).

Fortunately I still knew by heart, at that time of my first
talk most of the epic Storm in which Steerforth perished. I
came to David's taking his dead friend back to his mother's
home . . . '*the chamber where he lay I darkened last . . . I
lifted his leaden hand and held it to my heart . . . and all was
death and silence, broken only by his mother's moaning.*'

I became aware of noses being blown into khaki handker-
chiefs.

'If you could make them cry over *Steerforth*,' said Bernard
later (who obviously found it hard to believe), 'you *must* be a
genius.'

'Cross, because you were wrong!' I accused him.

Afterwards I talked to W.A.A.F.S. and W.R.N.S. anywhere
I was asked. About? Anything. Dickens's characters. H. G.
Wells's short stories. My friend Amy Johnson (a pioneer still
fresh in their minds) and the blue-bottle fly that had been her
comfort and the only other living thing within miles and miles
of lonely night-sky on her record flight to South Africa. Dan
Leno, as I'd seen him on the stage. A talk on the Six Men in a
Woman's Life . . .

Grape-vine rumour reached me that in some official quarters there had been haggling over the pay for speakers, instruc-

tional or as mere entertainment. Of me it was reported :

'She *has* no special subject. She appears to say anything that comes into her head to make the troops laugh.'

The reply from another Authority—'Anybody who can make the troops laugh in THIS climate deserves an extra guinea.'

I got it.

Presently they gave me a pink cardboard pass with *Adult Education for the Forces* on it. This was to show to sentries after I received orders to talk to men troops. I have it still, to witness if I lie. I went to Llanbedr, Barmouth, Harlech. At one of these stations, I forget which, I overheard an officer ask an N.C.O. afterwards,

'Men seem interested at all ?'

'Listened like mice, Sir. It was quite peculiar.'

I felt that, myself.

At the end of the War I *missed* this going about speaking to a large mixed audience.

That was when I started having an ambition.

Chapter Sixteen
Talk about Men

I

'And such a glorious day for it! . . . Fancy if it had been raining
. . . Don't *speak* of it; as it is, it couldn't be lovelier . . . And
think of the *treat* it'll be for them . . . And the rhododendrons
out! such a CHANGE from all those Factories and smoke—'

The scene was rural Wales at her late-spring-time best on a
radiant day of the—'forties or 'fifties?—everyone knows what
I am like about *dates*. Anyhow, it would be during those
decades before Continental tours at possible rates were
arranged for workers. Wales would be Quite a Trip.

The occasion was a special Women's Institute 'Do'. Organisers: certain members of a Welsh W.I. Guests: forty or more
representatives of a Club or Townswomen's Guild further
North.

'Such a *change* for them it'll be,' was the theme-song of the
organisers. 'After cooped up in those drab streets, and always
those Awful Old Fogs!'

The party had pilgrimaged in one of those great red
touring-coaches which picked us up over the border. I had
been included to give a little 'Talk', in the afternoon, as I'd
done to the W.I. in the War. 'About? Anything you like! Just
to fill up the interval before tea.'

There had been no interval in the blithe chatter that filled the coach as we drove along the coast-road to Barmouth. 'Trips' loosen tongues of the Touring through any countryside, any weather. Today sunshine smiled on every mile between the sea and the down-sweeping hillside verdant with uncurling bracken. I could hear my nearer fellow-passengers . . . comparing notes on hours at which alarm clock had been set overnight . . . these were no factory-workers, though. These were housewives, chatting about arrangements Back Home.

'Eh, I left all ready. . . . Our Emma'll see to that, she's seen to her Dad any time. After all, she's turned *eleven* . . . !'

Had we crossed the toll-bridge at Penmaenpool before lunch at a café en route? Chatter at tables compared meals on other trips. Now we'd arrived at that corner of the Caernarvonshire coast which is forever Italy—Or as like it as Architect Mr. Clough Williams Ellis can make it. Banished, the greys of native masonry, the old stone hedges . . . Colouring and slender spires as of Riva welcomed us . . . The verdict I heard later of a Caernarvonshire born man: *'Yes, very nice . . . but what it wants now is some nice big Welsh Chapel in the middle of it to pull it together, like.'*

We'd reached the show-piece. The highlight of the trip. 'Something for them to remember!' murmured one of the Organisers.

The rhododendron groves of Porth-Merion!

Groves we passed through on foot were at their utter peak. Out of the dark foliage of those shrubberies the rhodos glowed in glory: they offered great sunlit bouquets of colour: crimson, purple, vermilion, primrose—pinkish-white—

One or two of the guests—tweeded Madam President types —were keen gardeners. They produced pencils, little books, took notes. One of them enquired who was responsible for the planting and tending of all this? A master-hand! . . .

Does the modest shade of 'little old Blount' still flit in and out and about those groves because (like our Welsh grandmother's

spirit at her home Pantlludw) he *couldn't* be anywhere else?
He had known how these exotics from Persia and the Himalayas would acclimatise themselves here, as well as does the
commoner mauve sort that makes high hedges along the
Welsh roads and romps wild up our woodlands. These are
descendants of the Ponticum. Roman officers of the Occupy-
ing Legion stationed in Ancient Britain had rhododendron
plants sent over from the gardens of their Tiber-side villas. On
our misted mountain slopes, they have flourished through the
centuries. As will (let's hope) those newer importations to the
beauty now surrounding us.

'*Look* at those bushes,' (a visitor's voice pronounced it to
rhyme with rushes), 'Puts you in mind of that Park at—'

'*Beautiful*,' said another to friends in a group. They had
paused by a tall spread of my favourite, *Pink Pearl*, that
Voluptuous Blonde among rhodos. Some find her too flam-
boyant. They prefer her neighbour, the pinkish-white Frag-
rantissima . . . But the group had halted, listening to the last
speaker . . . Backed by the full blooms against the cobalt sky
she was describing, not the rhododendron, but the spring-
cleaning of her old Auntie in Yorkshire. 'That front-parlour
of hers. *Beautiful* she'd got it . . . She went over and over, did
Auntie. Had it looking as if everything had come straight out
of shop . . . Well, she hadn't hardly been sat down in kitchen
for her cuppa tea,' the voice of the speaker went on, 'than
there was a ring at the front-door. "Nay!" says Auntie, "I'd
locked up all fast *in case*!" Tip-toed upstairs to the bedroom
and there she'd stopped in the cold till she'd heard them try
at back, find it locked and bolted, and go away, thinking they'd
made sure Mrs. Unthank must be from home . . . "Visitors?"
she says, "when I'd got everything *nice*?" She says, "I wasn't
going to have any visitors' boots tramping in all over my
clean"—'

Striking contrast to the ways of any gregarious gossip-loving
Welsh housewife! Can't you hear her welcoming—'Come In,
Mrs. Jones-bach! . . . I was going to make a cup of tea this
minute. You'll excuse the kitchen, bit of a mess?'

As we walked slowly along I realised how different were

these guests. They had been accustomed as eleven-year-olds to cope with House and Dad. They not only kept front-rooms *'Beautiful'* and back-kitchens innocent of 'Mess'. Super-cooks they would be; their suet-puddings would melt in the mouth, having taken as much thought and time to make as a film-star's face ...

II

Now here we were, in the white-washed village hall. It was the interval before tea, which I was there to fill up with a little Talk. I stood on the platform in front of the square table with the accounts-book, the book for the Minutes and the jar of roses and pinks. Madam (my country-woman) President introduced me ...

... A flop. That'll be me. I was thinking rapidly. Spoilt by speaking to Welsh audiences who always *enjoy* a speech even if it's not by themselves. These'll *criticise* ... They may not care about rhododendrons, but if it came to running a house—! Solomon's Virtuous Women would have nothing on them. Just to look at these—

I scanned the rows of pleasant, sensible North Country faces, looking expectantly up at me—makes me feel such a *mere* story-teller.

Still! Most of these were from the same end of the Kingdom as my ever-to-be-missed In-laws who'd liked me. And even Solomon's model wife and mother, who never took a moment off from the Chores must sometimes have longed for a Nice Sit Down and a Change of Subject.

'Well, Ladies,' I began, feeling oh, how mere! 'I see I am down on the programme—'

There was no programme, but this topic had pleased my Service girls during the War.

'—down on the programme to give a little talk about *Men*.'
Ah! This went? Forty faces smiling as one.

Immediately I felt less mere.

'However,' I continued impromptu, 'in view of the country-side we have explored, it might be of greater interest to our visitors, if the subject were changed to—*The Flowering Shrubs of North Wales.*'

Our visitors had *had* those shrubs. Walked miles through them. Faces falling like one. Mouths turning down.

'On second thoughts,' I had the grace to be ashamed of this leg-pull, 'I don't feel I am sufficiently well-up in all these long Latin *names* they have. So I will, if I may? stick to the original subject : *About Men.*'

Mouths turning up again.

I'd made sure this time that unless our driver turned up for a cup of tea at the end, there wasn't a man in the house.

Once, at a large W.I. gathering in . . . I'd dropped a shaming clanger. Addressing an apparently all feminine audience I'd said,

'Those who are, like some I know, disappointed because their first-born is *"only a girl"* must remember the country saying, "Any boy can get a boy but it TAKES A MAN TO GET A GIRL." '

At the end a tall fellow—'Press' or 'Accounts' I suppose? had risen from a corner at the back to announce cheerfully,

'Well, I was glad to hear from our lecturer that *I'm a better man than I thought I was!* Last week we had a little daughter!' (How they'd all laughed.)

'There are Six Men in a Woman's life,' I now told our visitors. Some of them looked a bit surprised at that 'six'? 'Men from whom she'll learn facts that are going to influence her life and character. Women are the Adaptable Sex.' (Never mind there being several types listening whom nothing on earth could shift from their own ways.) 'Women have *to put up* with more than men do. So they *learn*. I was once told by a man on a boat—' (That's the place where men talk endlessly to women: the only way a woman can get away is by springing up from her deck-chair and flinging herself over the ship's rail into the sea.)

K

'Any intelligent woman learns three useful new things from every fresh man she meets.

'The FIRST MAN comes very early on—Please look at this picture of him.' I made as if handing them a Christmas Number coloured supplement. 'A hefty young tough between twenty and thirty. In a rumpled sports' jacket. He is on hands and knees. Face proudly beaming and flushed from galloping in that position round and round the room. Astride his back sits a curly-headed moppet of two-and-a-bit. She wears a white, cutlet-frill of a frock, the shortest possible white socks, and tiny strapped slippers of scarlet kid.'

(The accepted wear for little girls at that date. Absurdly feminine and pretty it looked. Nowadays of course she would be in small-sized anorak and jeans, with hair left as long as a boy's.)

'One small paw clutches her charger's hair. The other brandishes the dog's lead as a riding-switch. The title of this picture, ladies, is *"Daddy's Girl."* '

A recognisably popular image. They saw it. They liked it. The tweeded Madam President slewed her head slightly to one side with a reminiscent smile. The woman next her nodded a terribly 'Sunday' purple hat. Could both of them have been Daddy's Girls?

How singularly unlike—I've told you of my own Father's attitude towards the Very Young of the Species until they reached 'a reasonable age'?

Flash-back—Esgair.

Father, in his 1912 knickerbocker suit and fishing hat emerges, preoccupied-looking, out of the veranda. Pulls up at the sight of unattended pram (his first grandson's) on the terrace. Demands: 'Who is looking after this Child? Because I'm not.' Legs it away, hurriedly.

No time to explain how different Father was later. Let the audience keep the picture of young Daddy, well under the thumb, small as a picked shrimp! of the fairy-Queen on his back. With my caption—'It's from her father that a Woman Learns she has the Whip-hand over Man!'

I turned to MAN TWO: Brother. He teaches her to keep Her Place.

Odd this sounded, when already Woman's Place was coming to mean where she chooses to keep herself.

'Brother tells her that Dad may be crazy about her, but who else was going to look at A Thing like Her? "Give a squint at yourself in the glass." Let Brother grow up a bit. The merciless Tease, inventor of hurting nicknames, the *Bully* will then evolve into the *Pal*. The girl sits up for him when he comes in late. They talk. He can give her the masculine point of view without sex-jealousy, without any glamouring-up Sex-Appeal. Sister can turn to Brother for help in a spot. Money-trouble. Even Young Man-trouble. Brother is a rock-tomb for her confidences.'

This had gone well with war-time Service-girls. They'd brothers fighting overseas...

I told them the true story of a fellow-member of my London Club who had *ten* brothers. She was good-looking, good-company. Had heaps of masculine attention, proposals. At forty-five, she remained unmarried. Why?

'Well, though I've known crowds of men not one of them measured up to being as fine as "the Boys".'

Audience-reaction to this—

There's silliness for you. Missing chances because she didn't see a chap as good as them, and they, I'll be bound, all married, homes of their own, and She on the shelf, just Old Maid Auntie to their kids! DAFT.

I passed on to

'MAN THREE in a Woman's Life: the Admirer.' Faces brightened.

'Ladies, haven't most of us at some time been told to *"Wait until Mr. Right comes along"*?'

Laughter. Not a woman in that hall, married or single, English or Welsh, hadn't been maddened by that smug cliché.

I quoted the Cockney music-hall song :

> *Mr. Right, Mr. Right! it is turning pretty late*
> *and there ain't a sign of him yet.*
> *But Cheer up, girls! He is getting on his boots,*
> *And he'll soon be here, you bet.*

But who is Mr. Right?
His best point remains what he ISN'T.
He isn't the daily round of the *same* things. Same faces at the breakfast-table—Dear familiar faces, how you'd miss them if they were no longer there! Still, there they are. Same tiresome reminders *to pop round to the sweep and tell him etc.*

Mr. Right isn't The Family. He's the visitor who notices you're looking smart in a new frock. Which of course starts you being better-looking. Presently he becomes the Taker-out. You get on. Then . . . It depends. The tempo wanes. But— Cheer up, girl! Mr. Right *is* getting on his boots, preparing to become MAN THE NEXT . . .

A too-serious subject is better treated lightly. So—MAN FOUR, the Husband, is a Creature of Slogans. Trademarks. One is: 'Ready, Dear? Time we're off.' Dear *isn't* ready. Zip-trouble! With luck, Husband is a Zip-King, otherwise it's Hey for a cover-all coat and trust in some helpful woman where you're due.

Another Trademark: 'ARE YOU UPSTAIRS, Dear?' Of course Dear is upstairs. She has just got the baby 'down' and she's waiting till he's 'off'. *Must* she leave him, and hurry to greet and feed whichever out of that herd of trampling trumpeting elephants Husband has brought home? She will. Even while she asks herself WHY did I marry that man?

She knows, though. It's because he brought her what the French called the Three Essential Wedding-Gifts—Illusion, Security, and a Child. (Even if he did wake that Child up to yell). He was Mr. Right.

'What about Mr. Wrong? MAN FIVE? Or I should say MAN
FOUR.—He generally comes before Mr. Right—and *what* a
Charmer.'

He doesn't charm her family? Much she cares. The girl's
day is made or blacked-out according to whether or not she
sees him. Moth-like she flutters round the telephone. Dates he
keeps more than make up for when he calls—'*Madly sorry,
sweet, but this evening's too tricky.' 'Sorry, darling, I'll try to
make it Thursday! . . . Lunch on the dot!*' She has been
warned! She doesn't hear a word of warning. She 'hears a
rhapsody'. (His voice). After Thursday she spends hours
refusing to believe he's changed, *nor taste the latter kisses like
the first.* More ages of waiting. At long last the call, '*Sorry,
my dear, I've got to go.*' Somewhere else . . . To someone else
. . . Exit Charmer, the man who can make a woman's Life
into a feast, then leave her to wash up and to empty the ash-
trays.

After she's put the shattered pieces of her heart together
she'll have learned to appreciate Mr. Right.

'She will have learned something about herself!' Been given
an awareness of how human passion can have lain latent in
the heart . . . I didn't say this. I was remembering lines—wish
I knew who by?—that express the force of Mr. Wrong. I
quoted them aloud.

> '*He's spoken words you never can forget.
> He showed you stars you never saw before.
> How wise if you'd not let him in—And yet
> How poor, if you had sent him from the door!*'

Fresh audience-reaction?

They were listening intently. Not to me! In that unlikely
place the 'feel' rose that to all these women stars had been
shown, words uttered, even if only in fancy! that they would
not forget. Does one never know what may be inside hearts?

But now figures at the back of the hall rose and disappeared.

Walking out on me? Only to see to the plates of sandwiches, cake and traditional Welsh *bara brith* (raisin bread, dark, nutty-flavoured, delicious). I accelerated on MAN SIX in a woman's life. 'One type of woman would "boil the rest of the family to make Soup for the Son".' (North-country saying picked up from my In-laws). 'Unfair that a woman will do less for the most attentive husband than she will for the neglectful son! Even, when that son comes of courting age she panics . . . "Some little So-and-So will be after my Boy!" Instead of being thankful that soon, now, there'll be someone else to do the Boy's everlasting laundry!'

Chinkles of crockery on tin trays from the kitchen at the side of the hall. Tea coming now. Cheers!

'End on the UP-beat,' as my young granddaughter instructed me. I'd always tried to do so before I knew it was *called* that. So, for the last word on Sons—

'One can only say of them, as of men in general and particular—

> *"Bad as you are, we love you;*
> *Bad as you are, we love you;*
> *And thank your lucky star*
> *That when you come back to Tipperary*
> *We'll love you as bad as you are." '*

III

Back at Aberdovey.

'No dinner for me, please. Just bara llaeth.' (Bread and milk.)

Zoë Williams, the sea-captain's daughter in whose house in the terrace facing the mouth of the Estuary, we then lived, had it ready. She knew it was all Mrs. Oliver ever wanted after she'd been away preaching.

My husband surfaced out of his *Times* cross-word puzzle.

'Where've you been today?'

'Porth Meirion. Oh, if you'd seen the *Colour* of those rhododendrons—!'

'What were you "preaching" about?' he asked with the mixture of poker-faced resignation, mock apprehension and indulgent curiosity with which he treated my sorties and those loose Celtic analogies [*sic*.] 'Celebrities you've met?'

'No. Men, sort of.'

'Did they like it?'

'I *think* so.' Between spoonfuls of bara llaeth I told him about the vote of thanks. 'One of the visitors got up and said in a voice like Ethel's, "On be'alf of Runcorn" (or wherever it was), "I wish to thank for the kind hospitality we've received here today. Tea. Trip. Scenery. And ree-marks about men—all champion." '

The poker-faced Yorkshire Expression broke up into that smile which makes you wonder *Why can't all of them, always, be like that?*

Just as well, perhaps, that they can't.

Chapter Seventeen
Maid-Service

I

Two words that are *out,* now, of today's speech—'Maid-Service'.

A few of us can have flash-backs to a time when there were maids. Everywoman, as we knew her, had at least *a* maid. It was a matter-of-course that she, Everywoman, paid another woman to live in her house and do the chores that Everywoman now has to do for herself. (In addition, perhaps, to her having a job herself outside the home, but that is another subject.) Though some are lucky enough to have 'Help'.

Imagine if you can? what a modern, well-paid, and independent young Household Help would say when asked to accept domestic conditions that are still within the memory of man—and woman?

To be *In Service* meant that you lived in, as a matter-of-course, sleeping in some draughty attic. But then only if you could show you could be trusted in A Good Place by bringing with you a written 'character' to state that you were Hardworking, An Early Riser, Thoroughly Reliable, Honest, Truthful, and Clean. By the way, even 'good' houses were for a long time minus a bathroom. The maid (you) fetched water for the young ladies' saucer-baths, carting it in a king-sized, gleaming copper hot-water can—haven't you seen them in antique shops?—up probably more than one flight of stairs . . . *Weigh the vessel up!* I don't know how they managed it.

Some employers allowed their maids one afternoon off a week. I suppose this was the only time the poor girls had—if that! to see what we now matily recognise as *Boy-friends*. In those days the idea of *Young Men* (for maids) was heavily discouraged.

'No followers' was no joke, but a *stipulation*. And one not wrapped in the mists of antiquity, either.

I know someone—who-knew-someone—who took part in this (to you no doubt unbelievable) Incident.

The servants [*sic*] of the house were lined up in readiness to follow their mistress to Church.

She perceived, to her wrathful horror, that the youngest of them had fastened into her otherwise chastely suitable Sunday bonnet A Pink Rose! Such vanity, in a servant! Why, it might be—possibly was?—a symptom somehow connected with that distasteful and forbidden factor *A Young Man*.

'Go back at once and TAKE THAT OUT,' was the order. Trembling, the poor little maid obeyed.

An under-servant was in those days less than the dust beneath the barouche wheels.

Even much later on—Imagine the reaction of any valued Household Help of today if she could be confronted with *an old-fashioned kitchen* of the same sort as Michael Flanders' *kitchen like we had before*. The dank stone floor. The cavernous black kitchen-range. The buckets in which to lug in coal from the yard. (Even empty, you'd think it would take a strong man to lift them.) The noisome scrubbing brushes for use on the floors. Those zinc pails. Those smelly great bars of yellow soap. That unappetising sink. Saucepans big enough to boil an emu in. Dust-pans and brushes as if for the excavations at Caerleon. Brooms—the very broomsticks thick as if constructed for the use of witches only. All kitchen equipment so ponderously *heavy*. Made *to last*.

Thank Heaven and two Social Revolutions it has not lasted.

II

War, and Peace—Peace in our time—brought about the mistress doing kitchen-work that was once the department of the maid if not the staff, and she wasn't going to stand for doing it in *that* kind of kitchen.

Hence labour-saving devices. Lightness is all. Hence the invention of dish-washers, washing-machines for the wealthier households. Plastic ware, charmingly coloured, in place of zinc, iron and the heavier-than-lead implementing of other days. Think of them, you who moan nostalgically for everything in the Past. Think of the changes *there*—And so, enough of *that*.

Of the maids that I knew personally, two remain memorable.

Lydia, the very Welshy-est of the North Welsh in ways, dark looks and speech before maids learnt English as it would be spoken today; and Ethel, the no-less typical 'lassie from Lancasheer'.

III

Lydia comes first.

Her pretty name may have been a hangover—one from Ancient Rome during the Occupation of Segontium, centuries before that town became Caernarvon. I knew an Italian Lydia later, who served, as 'daily', the holiday-flats in a French coastal-village. A note on the lift conveyed *that* Lydia's polite, laboriously written request that the gates should be kept shut. *Ferme la censeur sivous ple!* Her French was as individual as some of *our* Lydia's English.

Our Lydia worked for our parents when they lived in Caernarvon. Most of us eight children were at school, two of the boys in 'Caernarvon County' (since then the Grammar School).

Domestic service was already a very different thing from that offered to the little maid of the Pink Rose in Her Bonnet

Scandal. Lydia was a friend. Was this because Wales was always (as the Americans said of Edward the then Prince of Wales) *kind of democratic*? Yet Lydia had with it a curious streak of feudalism, her own standard of class. Of an English family who had bought a large castellated house in the neighbourhood, Lydia reported the gossip. 'Lot o' money they got. *Lot* o' money. But not like you, they aren't.'

Certainly *not* like us, we thought ruefully. *Can't afford it,* summed up too many of the things we should have liked if we had thought much about it.

Lydia, however, said further of these wealthy ones—'Not *The High Gentry,* like you.'

This became a long-lived family joke.

Another of Lydia's winged words was her answer to a teenage brother who had bagged and brought home a rabbit.

'Did you find the shot, Lydia?'

'Yes, Mr. D'Arcy!' (note the ceremonious address to the school-leaver).

'Where was it?'

'In his s' ARM, sir!'

Never a smile at any idiom of Lydia's, though. Touchier than the average native Welsh—which is saying much!—she would be angrily hurt at any suggestion that we'd laughed at her. She could not take criticism of anything to do with her or her belongings, her activities. At any hint of blame she was offended. 'I vex' and 'fend' was the phrase. She flared up. Gave instant notice in the words, 'I go tonight!'

Lydia stayed with our family for years.

IV

Ethel was of a later date in our lives. I came upon her in London when I was (with difficulty) starting to earn my living. I was writing. I had left the Slade and Paris. My Scholarship there had finished and didn't seem to promise further use. Ambition to be an artist had left me. All I wanted was not to be at home, as an expense. Also I *must live* a more exciting life in London, like all my best friends, and be *of* if not *at* the still dear Slade. I wrote virtuously domestic articles and short stories for two of the women's weeklies—*Forget-me-not* and *Home Chat*. As windfalls I got the occasional illustration to do; the odd set of pen-and-ink advertisements for Scott's Emulsion.

Ethel Core was another of the world's workers who had abandoned her first idea of the Job in her Life.

Flashback of Ethel, in her pre-War teens, with shrewd blue eyes, sharply clear features, a knob of light-gold hair worn on the top of her head, a pale, and pretty face, and the Shape of a Twiggy-to-come. She had *been* on the stage. Of a fit-up repertory company. In Victorian melodrama. I have been privileged to be the only audience, when I made One at a special performance by Ethel, declaiming her lines ('*Scoundrel! You dare to breathe these words into the ears of a Wife and Mother on the very threshold of the House of Gord?*') with what *brio* ! . . .

Today she might have become a Discovery of that genius of producers, Miss Joan Littlewood. Ethel was photogenic, too. If she had bleached that hair to a paler blondeur and worn it down her spine, had re-drawn her mouth, had acquired fake eyelashes, and been trained to roll glances like blue marbles on a white plate, she might have blossomed into a new Lulu, or even a Cilla Black? She could sing, too.

Not fancying the Theayter for long (*lot o' nonsense!*), Ethel switched to domestic Service in London. Cockney acquaintances made fun of her Lancashire accent and pronunciation. Ethel did not, as Lydia would have done, flare up in offence. She hit back, laughing, '*Anyways, I don't call a booket a PILE!*'

After some party at the other end of London from my room in Pimlico, my habitat at the time, Ethel, leaning nonchalantly against the front door as she was seeing me out, asked, 'Miss Ruck, shall I be coming to work for you when you're married to Mr. Onions?'

'Who on earth said I was *going* to marry him?'

'Nobody,' said Ethel. 'But when I see shells I can guess eggs.'

Ethel (after her guess of eggs had proved correct) might not have provided conventional 'maid-service', but she was to be a treasured jewel as cook. Her suet pudding, specially, melted in the mouth. It was given as much loving care and time to make as a film-star's face. She came with us to help out during a visit to Wales.

The Lancashire lassie's comment on our nation, 'Nice people! Do anything to make a person feel at home . . . funny thing about the Welsh, though. Always full and plenty to eat but never a hand's-turn o' work done to get it!'

Back in the Hampstead Ponds flat she became a devoted second attendant after 'the little boys' were there, staying on even after she married George. (I don't believe I heard his surname.)

Ethel introduced the subject by telling me 'He's only a working-man, but he's very fond of me, so there we are.'

They had a little girl to be called Ethelberta, 'after her mother and your mother,' I told the boys, who were still quite small. 'I'm to be her godmother.'

Our elder son asked, 'Will she be our god-sister?'

The younger one looked at the small bundle in the white woolly matinée-jacket, threaded, correctly, with pink ribbon for a girl, and asked it politely,

'Do you like pink?' No answer? 'Can't it *speak*?'

'She will when she's older.'

They moved to the North where George had the opportunity of better-paid work, but there little Ethelberta did not live long enough to learn to talk.

Ethel wrote thanking me for money I'd sent (no such thing as Interflora Service in those days) for flowers. 'I bought a beautiful harp from you for Ethelberta.'

The flash-back I keep of that short life is set at her christening at Hampstead.

Our two boys in sailor-suits were taken to Church for the first time. They stood, one each side of me, unusually well-behaved (awed?) and silent. It came to the Padre praying, 'Our Father which art in Heaven—'

At these familiar words which I had managed to teach them, I felt a tug at each side of my skirt. I heard from each of our sons a loud, pleased, recognising whisper

'He *knows* it!'

'*He* knows it!'

To me this seemed to shed a side-light on Theology.

Even as I recall it there glimmers up a sort of hope that in some Hereafter, in some perhaps higher state of Evolution, soul may meet liberated soul, once consigned by him to the Outer Darkness made inevitable by any form of divergent Faith and may realise, 'He knew it! He, too, knew the Light!'

Chapter Eighteen
A Wreath for the In-Laws

I

A safe bet to win the hearts of Welsh folk is to fall in love with Wales—like my little Yorkshire mother-in-law whom I called 'Mam'.

We were at Esgair. The old house was 'between tenants'. My father suggested that we should move in for a break from London—'and why not have Mrs. Goodliffe for a visit, if she'd care to come?'

She came. Small mauve-trimmed bonnet on her white springy hair. Stiff linen collar up to her firm little chin. Grey-blue glance that could take in most things without delay and with a smile.

We prevented her, almost by main force! from starting in to give a thorough spring-cleaning to all the rooms, which had of course been left in charge of family retainer, dear old Shan who came up daily. So during the mornings we, my husband and I, were busy with our '*work*, as they call it!' Mam's term for earning our bread. I was writing eminently domestic articles or a serial for one of the women's weeklies of that era. Oliver Onions was 'at'—which of his spine-chilling ghost-stories? Esgair was full of ghosts, but for generations before ours. Mam meanwhile pottered happily about outside, on the terrace. Snipping dead heads off the roses. Going down the short cut between the trees, with our letters, to Pantperthog—

surely the smallest village in the Principality? In that mere slice of a post-office she exchanged weather-forecasts with Lydia-the-Post or wasn't it Lydia then? I forget. Mam lingered to chat sociably with any who came in. These sessions were enjoyed, I think, by both sides. Through Mam I learnt more than I'd ever known about my home-hamlet.

Afternoons were given to taking Mam for drives. No cars in existence yet? Not available, anyhow. We had the old carriage, comfortable enough in spite of the horse-hair that sprouted here and there out of the upholstery. The horse took his own time to clop, clop along. Unlike the tempo of any car in which any of Mam's grandsons would ever set foot, there was leisure for her to look out from this side of this shandrydan to the other, taking in the scenery. Evan Rees, Shan's husband, drove: glad to show a stranger a 'little bit of the country, like'. Father said Evan was the most intelligent man he knew. Evan hadn't bothered to learn to read or write. He was an unerring reader of character. A green-fingered gardener. A tireless worker on six days of the week. A chapel-goer who'd get every word of the Minister's sermon by heart and could repeat it verbatim to any challenger.

Down Esgair's long steep drive he took us, past the lattice-windowed lodge Lliwdy, inhabited by Bodo Leis, out of Esgair gate.

On! The road between the deep valley (where you now, looking down, see a mushroom growth of holiday caravans) and that hillside heaped to the sky-line with purple pyramids of slate.

'Nobody *working* there?'

'Not now, Mam. Disused, most of them.'

Who could foresee the years when those same pyramids were to mask hiding-places for the nation's treasures, buried deep under the slate? No breath of War's disruption, slaughter, stinking horror came to us on the soft breath of that afternoon. Flash-backs show a lovely little country, oddly foreign to anything beyond Offa's Dyke, but secure in its protection, where all was peace that seemed set to last forever, like the supremacy of the British Empire.

Carefully Evan took the horse down the precipitous hill, still untouched by any smoothing, white-lined road improvements. It branched away from the turning that leads up to the ascent of Cader Idris. Skirted Tal-y-llyn, smooth as glass. Near the bank Evan pointed with his whip—nesting swans.

Always the same place, at this time of year.

Tyn-y-Cornel, not yet a smart Hotel Restaurant with a sunshine-porch where the menu is brought for the inspection of visitors sipping sherry, but a simple little fishing-inn reflected in the lake.

Mountains opposite sweep down towards the water. We leave them. Past Bird Rock, towering above the farm Gesail that nestles cosily below.

Mam's little bonnetted head and white curls turn this way, that way.

'Beautiful' . . . The Yorkshire Dales are grand, but all this is new to her. 'Eh, it's beautiful,' she says to the right, to the left.

Towyn. Past its square-towered, 600-year-old Church, its Market-hall. Through Aberdovey, thrusting its ancient pier like a bather's foot into the rising tide, and so home.

When she left us Mam said it was the best holiday she had ever had.

There had not been too many holidays for Mam. Take the start of her wedded life—

II

A funny thing happened to my mother-in-law on her way back from Church where she, Alice Emily Fearnley (then touchingly young! her husband's pet-name for her was 'Tem') had just been married.

Her bridegroom was arrested.

Yes! I do mean arrested by the Police.

If only coloured photography had been invented by that time, think of the wedding-group it would have given us!

Framed by the porch of Birstal Church. Bride in traditional snowstorm of white with orange-blossom and bouquet. Bride-

L

groom in unfamiliar frock-coat with choking high collar. Surround of relatives, friends, spectators all at the ready to throw rice. Suddenly, making their way up through the crowd, Police in the uniform of 1847 with the announcement: 'George Frederick Onions, I arrest you on the charge of arson—'

'*Him!* Who'd never been able to lay a fire in his life, let alone get one going,' as Mam declared with a laugh of merry scorn when she told me the story long afterwards.

It was no laughing matter on that October morning of her wedding-day. Circumstantial evidence was black against him, and he was taken off in custody to be jailed without bail.

How my Welsh Nain, that expert on family-history, would have revelled in this case! Tirelessly she would have dug out all the details, the 'come-from' of the real delinquent and what had happened before his crime was discovered and at what Assizes he was brought to justice.

All I know about it was what my Mother-in-law told me. What seemed to have stayed most clearly in *her* mind is that she had, on the day after the wedding, to take her husband's dinner to him in prison, if you please.

I can see 'Tem', less in sorrow than in anger, marching up to those grim gates. Back very erect. Head held high in new trousseau bonnet over curls—then brown. Small gloved hands clutching covered basket containing meal for captive mate. I don't know of what it consisted, but I can swear it would have been kept expertly hot, and that it tasted as good as it smelt. Mam was ever 'a grand cook'.

As for the young (alleged) fire-raiser my father-in-law, bookish and delicate, I never knew him. He had died before I made my way, via London, Paris, and Wales, into his family.

Nor, of course, had I set eyes on his father, my husband's grandfather, the Parson. I *heard* a good deal about the Reverend George Onions from Mam.

'A *Terror*, love,' she told me. 'Everybody scared stiff of him. Strict with his sons? . . . My word! . . . And his wife? Couldn't move . . . He was all that particular about her dress being suitable for a clergyman's wife—'

(I thought of the timid English lady depicted in *Punch* who told the milliner in Paris that she wanted a hat *'très tranquil'* because she was *'la femme d'un Curé'*.)

A right Terror he was. She never in her life called him anything but 'Mr. Onions'!

She might well have loved him though . . . ?

My husband kept an old photograph, taken from a portrait of the Terror as a young man. A high collar—not a 'dogger'. A vista of white shirt and black satin stock the size of an antimacassar. Nice-looking, the face. Clean-shaven. Curling hair. Sensitive hands, one holding a rolled-up paper. Notes for a sermon? More likely the score for some piece of music. Music! —That had been his passion, first and last.

'I'll tell you what he did for years, my dear,' said Mam. '*After* he was young. Oh yes, getting *on* he was. Settled down years, the very-much-respected Reverend George Onions in his own country parish—'

And Mam went on to tell me how he—'here, this is another photograph of him . . .'—It showed him grown portly, alas! whiskered, and solemn—He used to walk the fifteen miles from his parish to Bradford every year, when they were giving *Messiah* in the Town Hall. There he would stand up in the gallery at the back. Never anywhere else. He had the score of the Oratorio with him and followed every note. When it came to the Choruses (the wonderful *Hallelujah Chorus* was his favourite) he joined in and sang, with the Choir, from where he stood.

When it was over he'd go but without a word to a soul. And walk the fifteen miles back to his parish. 'Right Yorkshire,' summed up Mam with a chuckle. 'He was a Character. Right Yorkshire!'

III

When she stayed with us at the 'Ponds flat' we had in Hampstead she liked it less than Wales.

She was kept uneasy by thoughts of 'That *Hoist*' as she called the obsolete buttery-hatch out of our kitchen into the living-room. Suspect! 'Too handy for *burglars*!'

Gravely her son assured her that burglars wouldn't worry about flats like ours. They knew where to look for valuables, jewellery, priceless silver and stuff. Burglars had got every promising house in Hampstead carefully X-rayed.

Mam's *look* at this Mocker! All her children teased her a good deal. Mam could take it. Had taken worse things.

When, still young, she was left a widow with three children, she was very hard-up, living in some back-street in Bradford. She had called upon great friends of her late husband's sure that they would find her an occupation, some means of helping the little family out. The friends were just about to sit down to their dinner. *They put it back into the oven to wait till she went.*

This, when one of her girls told me of it, left me speechless!

It had not soured Mam : it gave her a more realistic view of life, perhaps. She had been re-married for some years when I met her.

In Yorkshire we stayed at Bank Top, the bungalow in Baildon, near 'Ilkla Moor' of the song.

Here, and everywhere else where we got together, the Interfering, Definitely Disliked Mother-in-law of Music-Hall lyrics remained a solar Myth, as far as I was concerned.

As for my sisters-in-law, things were all right from the word go, I think. They were as lively as the gayer types of Welsh people, but with a drier, slightly wry of humour. They were practical and efficient. Shrewder, better-balanced than I could hope to be. Wiser, in some ways, in their generation. We had had such different childhoods, outlook on life . . . They appeared to find me something *new*! Was it the charm of Novelty, or the Attraction of Opposites? We got on without thinking why, without even thinking whether we did or not. Which is a sign of Getting on Well.

The younger Miss Onions ('It's all O in our family,' she warned me) owned an obese, shuffling, snuffling bulldog called Obbis, short for Robinson. Echo of a trick she taught him.

'Obbis! What's that Word drunk men say?'

Obbis would respond with a hoarse grunt and snuffle which sounded uncannily like a drunkard's oath.

Obbis's mistress had a unique way of dealing with her brother if he emerged from work to the family tea-table still wrapped in one of his anti-social, absorbed, absent-eyed writer's moods.

She would twist her features into a gargoyle grin. Snatching a shiny tea-spoon from a saucer she would hold it, as one does to reflect a baby, close up to her brother's aloof face and cry, 'Laugh for the spoon, Olly! Laugh, *laugh*!'

And he, strugglingly reluctant, would be forced out of that mood into laughter at his sister's clowning.

'Emmie, you fool!'

In the Shakespearean sense she

> *was our fool.*
> *And (she) will never make us laugh again.*

How these characters would be missed from the Plays! How missed, in daily life....

The elder sister, Agnes, was a trained nurse. She came to us for all her days off in London where she worked in various Hospitals. In a lunatic ward. In the slums (pre-World War One). She was terse about 'conditions'.

'They go on at *The Poor* for being so feckless and dirty and untidy,' said Aggie. 'The *Poor* have darned little to be clean and tidy *with*!' We put her to lie down after she'd come to us from night duty, gave her a good tea and read aloud to her our letters from home.

All Mam's letters, to say that she was sending a fowl from Reggie's farm, or warm socks she'd knitted for her son, hoped that 'Berta *wrapped up* well in this bitter weather!' (She knew I didn't), and ended

> 'With the same old love
>   MOTHER'

Most families make affectionate mock of their Grown-Ups? pet clichés. We did; even of Mam's same old love. (Does she think we're scared it's gone off since last week?)

The slogan with which Mam met any problem was 'A way will open!'

'Where TO?' we would enquire.

'Nay, there's no knowing yet; but *a way will open.*'

Agnes would shake her head as if baffled.

Fair-haired, grey-blue-eyed, light-skinned like her brother and sister, she was, I think, more akin to Oliver Onions in mind.

'She's much cleverer than I am,' he declared to me.

She was devoted to him. Enormously proud of his work. Amused with me. Glad when I produced nephews for her.

Mam of course spoilt the little boys shamelessly, inventing a line of baby-talk fantastic beyond any I'd heard.

War-time was to find Aggie's slim shape grey-uniformed with the traditional scarlet-bordered cape of the Queen Alexandra's Nursing Service on duties over in France, but still a visitor to us on all her short leaves. Her knapsack bulged with packages of French coffee, of nougat, special soap—luxuries which in that *first* year of World War I, she was permitted to bring over to us, her rationed kin.

I can hear the shrill cry of greeting from her youngest nephew (who was to fly, R.A.F. in the next war) of : 'Auntie Aggern-nurse!'

Her professional job she took with the utmost seriousness. Off duty she was her light-hearted, shrewd, family self, regaling us with descriptions of 'that Ritzy Paris Pub'—the Hotel which had been turned over to wounded British troops, and of the posh (and wealthy) feminine visitors.

'You ought to see the Helper we've won,' was one of her reports. 'A beauty. An Irish lad; very young. Wound in the shoulder. I've put him to sit out on the first floor balcony. Nice white bandage round his head. Nothing the matter with his head, of course. Nor with those eyes . . . And does it pull in the donations!'

Unexpectedly, this forthright, spirited North country

woman became—next to my life-long Irish inseparable—the closest woman friend I have made. She became less an In-law than a fifth sister. And so remained, even to the end, when she was running, with two partners, her own Nursing Home, Down Under, in Australia. To the end it was a very good and close relationship.

IV

Irony of Fate! Some people, with a clutch of in-laws who are mutually uncongenial—in other words hate each other's guts —live practically next door to each other for the rest of their days. Whereas to me, so sincerely attached to 'my Yorkshire Lot', not one of them is left.

A French verse has it—

> *Je vais où va toute chose*
> *Où va la feuille de la rose*
> *Et la feuille du laurier.*

(Roughly) :

> I go where each thing goes,
> The petal of the rose,
> The leaf of poet's bay.

One by one, they went, like leaves from the bough. The girls I never saw with grey in their hair. Their sturdy half-brother Reggie Goodliffe (we saw him off to the front, my husband and I after we ran in sweaters from Haverstock Hill, deserted in the early morning, down to Victoria Station). Kind-hearted little half-sister, Connie, among these, a latter-day Saint, a ministering Angel to the whole family—with one saving foible of vanity. . . . How she fretted, after a fever, because her head was shaved of her long brown hair! How pleased she was that it grew again, and in covetable natural curls.

And Mam, first of all to leave . . . Mam, who, when she heard repeated some doubtless well-deserved criticism of me, made that alarmingly dignified retort : 'Not a word against

Berta. She is the mother of my Grandsons, and as such she retains her place in My Heart.'

The same old love, in fact. (How could we ever have laughed at that phrase?)

V

Another phrase, often, but never irreverently quoted by the family, recurs to me. This was not Mam's, but dates from one of her own In-laws—that same 'Right Yorkshire' Old Character, the Reverend George Onions who, when no longer young, had tramped from his parish to Bradford to hear (and to take part in!) the Choir's glorious singing of *Messiah*, and would then make the fifteen miles on foot home.

Even that tough old Character came to an end of it, finally.

Relatives gathered round his bed thought he was asleep. Suddenly his eyes opened (*what, what had he seen . . . ?*) He sat bolt upright against his pillows, in a voice strong and clear as a young man's, called out: 'Hallelujah! *Don't wear black!*' and fell back.

To me those are the most strangely consoling, the most encouraging of last words.

Chapter Nineteen
S.O.S. to a Pirate

I

At the end of our conversation, I told Bill, my younger son :
'*You* are no help to your poor Mother!'

This was grossly untrue. In fact nothing could be *less* true
of this generously-helpful fellow—at any *other* time.

On this occasion I'd called for his help to get a situation, in
the story I was then writing, correct in the technical details.

He'd told me the *situation* was impossible. 'Couldn't
happen.'

Once upon a time this wouldn't have worried any 'romantic' novelist.

Take Ouida.

In *Under Two Flags,* published by Chapman and Hall in
1867, the gay little vivandière Cigarette, flask at seventeen-
inch waist, gallops on horseback into the broiling African
desert, there to serve brandy, neat, to the troops of the Foreign
Legion. . . . Pages on, she flings herself in front of the firing-
party drawn up to carry out the sentence of death passed on
the high-born English 'gentleman-ranker' she loves. I forget
the alleged crime. He was innocent. Reprieve would have
come . . . Seconds too late . . . but Cigarette has taken in her
own young breast the bullets aimed at his. She falls. Her dying
gasp to the firing-party—'*Ne pleurez-pas, les enfans* . . .'
(Don't cry, boys . . .)

An Army wept.

I cried unashamedly at the revival, decades later, of the dramatised stage-version.

Reviewers jeered at the novel? Ouida and her publishers could afford to let them jeer. Ouida's countless fans in the Army read *Under Two Flags* with serious avidity, as they read everything else she chose to create. She could get away with murder. She murdered the hampering facts. The Likely did NOT beat the mere Effective. The Effective beat the mere Likely, and could get away with it every time.

Not now!

Stories that are small beer compared with Ouida's strong wine have to be a hundred per cent *accurate about facts*. Verified. Otherwise carping readers write in and complain to publishers.

My son 'In the air' has often given me valuable tips about what NOT to put in any description to do with flying, and what to put instead.

He should know something about the sea, too.

Confidently I'd turned to Bill with my current plot about the triplet-babies.

'Their mother is aged 40, with two grown-up sons already out in the world. She herself is madly keen on her career as a portrait-painter. How could she, in these circumstances, cope with new babies—three of them at once? She can't. So, she doesn't. Keeping *one* of the "trips" (to please her husband) she gets the remaining two adopted in a rather hole-and-corner-way—'

My son wanted to know what I meant by hole-and-corner?

'It seemed that no Adoption Society would accept them. They were legitimate? Parents with adequate means? A perfectly good home? . . . So Mother appeals for help to God-father, a famous Harley Street gynaecologist with patients who desperately *want* babies. He *supplied* these two. Separately.'

'Sounds pretty illegal,' objected my son.

'I don't know why things I want for my stories always seem to be against some silly law?'

'I don't know why you always need something against the law to put into your stories?'

'Well, pass that. Nobody in their family-by-blood knows where these two adopted children get to. Or anything about them for the next 20 years. And *then*—'

I drew breath, then went on rapidly, 'Here's where I'm going to get a *Grand Finale*. All three of the triplets, grown-up, and looking exactly alike, of course! meet each other and their real parents for the first time.'

'How?'

'By a chain of coincidences that I've thought out. Rather craftily. One of the girls brings along her "childhood's sweetheart" for whom she's just dismissed her bridegroom-to-be. An odious man! She was only marrying him to get away from her adopted mother, whom she detested . . . She (triplet girl) was all ready to drive to the Church with her adopted father to give her away when, in the nick of time, the *first* lad of hers turns up, after years . . . Leaving the adopted father (a sympathetic character who's all for it) to cope with explanations. The couple drive off, at speed. She, radiant and still in her wedding dress and veil!, sits down to lunch with her first love, the two other triplets and her real mother. Enter, bewildered, her real father!—All for the first time for 20 years—happy together.'

'Where?'

'Oh, in the old home, I expect. Yes. That's how I shall arrange it.' I was pleased to notice that Bill *had* become interested in what happened. 'But about this boy—'

'Which boy?'

'The triplet-one. He'd been adopted twenty years back by a nice young American couple who were sailing with him to New York to their own parents. (The baby was to be a surprise for them. *They'd* kept it a secret.) This was at the start of the 1939 War. Their ship was one of the first to be torpedoed by a German submarine. She went down with every soul on board . . . *Not* before the young American had got the adopted baby-boy on to a raft and flung clear.'

'I doubt if—'

'Oh, that part's all right, I asked Commander T.' (a neighbour) 'and he admitted it just *could* have come off. . . . The raft, with something on it, was spotted by the Captain of the *Dilys Jones,* a small Welsh trading-vessel homeward bound to Liverpool Harbour.

' "Put out a boat," he orders. "Get that raft."

'The mate calls out "Capt'n, for God's sake, don't! It'll be a decoy! Trick of those Germans! Leave it!"

' "Who's Captain of this ship? PUT OUT A BOAT!"

'They do. Nothing to show where the baby is from—'

'Raft would have the ship's name on it.'

'This raft hadn't. The baby was wrapped in a cot blanket that was ditched at once. There he is, aboard. Washed. Fed with warm milk. Wrapped in an old clean flannel shirt of the Captain's, put to sleep on a pillow in a laundry-basket in the Captain's cabin. So far, so good. *Now* comes my difficulty, Bill. The thing is this. The Captain has to get that baby boy straight into his—the Captain's—home near Liverpool as soon as the ship docks. Without any holding up by Infant-Welfare-workers and committee-women from orphanages and those. He wants it for "the wife".'

'Haven't *they* any children, either?'

'Oh, yes! They'll be part of the story. Brothers and sisters for him . . . School age, those are,' I rattled on. I wanted to get the difficulty settled. 'You see, just before he sailed, their youngest *baby* had died. His wife had been fretting herself sick over that. (He was just about the same age as the boy-triplet.) And her husband feels sure that she would take the little castaway to her breast, and be comforted by having to look after him.—Well, so she does, but—' I didn't recount the scene where the Captain's wife insists on putting an advertisement in the *Liverpool Daily Post* in case some relatives of the little castaway are heart-brokenly mourning his imagined loss at sea. I'd *coped* with that. 'Just tell me how the Captain gets him ashore *unnoticed.*'

'He can't,' said my son. Just like that.

'Why not?'

'To begin with haven't you thought of the ship's log-book?

Every detail of that voyage would have been entered, every day. Latitude, longitude. Time of day skipper'd have to enter—'

'But if he *didn't*?'

'He *has* to . . . You haven't thought what the other ship's officers would have to say? The men who put out in the boat? The mate who warned him the raft might be a decoy? And when they dock . . . You haven't thought of the Immigration Laws?'

'*Were* there any, then?'

'Much tightened up after the outbreak of war. And—'

'Anything else?'

'Yes. The Customs Officers.'

'A baby a few weeks old, without so much as one "tiny garment" of his own, wouldn't have to go through *Customs*?'

'They have to go through the ship for anything dutiable. Wouldn't they hear something yelling its head off? First thing they'd find. In the Captain's cabin. Male baby—Unaccounted for. Not a stowaway. More serious than that. Might be Big Money involved for smuggling in the kid—*Whose?*—into this country. In war time. Apart from grave trouble for the skipper . . . And—oh, yes! Important to make sure if the kid's been immunised against this, that and the other.—Whisked over to the *Save the Children* lot. Dumped into a suitable Home—'

'*Ruining* my whole *story*!'

'I'm only telling you why it's impossible.'

This was where I decided: 'Bill, you're no help. You're too *law*-abiding, Bill . . .'

It then came to me who could tell me how to *get round* things. *He'd* got round plenty. Jail-breaking! Not out of ordinary prison but worse, prisoner-of-war Camp. Ship-wrecked! Half-drowned! Cast ashore without passport when he and one other fugitive were the only two white men on an island populated by an odd job-lot of every colour, creed and race. Made no difference *what* they were, this friend had told me once, 'all in the same boat, getting along fine together . . .'

I said now, 'I'll ask the Pirate.'

Meaning our Aberdovey celebrity Mr. Stan Hugill.

II

He is no ordinary pirate. That's my name for him.

You'd pick him out of a crowd the moment you saw him, which might be some moments *after* you'd heard his *ship-ahoy* voice making the Welkin ring. You'd think Who's *that* wild character? *Wild-looking*; actually he's in that highly responsible job at the Outward Bound Sea School. Pride of our village! Isn't it a grand experience for many town-dwelling lads to have taken that training-course in out-door pursuits between the mountains and the sea? Hasn't the School been visited by the Earl and Countess of Merioneth (better known as the Queen and Prince Philip). Stan Hugill, as bo'sun, is the right man in the right place. Of pupils who are leaving the Outward Bound for voyages to foreign parts, Stan has begged for copy of any sea-songs they come across. He wanted them to add to the ones he had himself acquired.

His collection of shanties, *Sea-songs of the Seven Seas*, is the classic work on the subject. It was the last present to me of my husband Oliver Onions, who thought highly of Stan. A broad-caster on his own subject, himself a singer of the songs. ('Ask Mr. Hugill to modulate his voice a bit, it's set things vibrating here,' requested a radio producer in another room.) Stan is also a painter of sea-scapes, and of the old sailing-vessels *Off to Mother Carey where she feeds her chicks at sea!*

His home, now that after his adventurous sea-faring days he's settled down with a comely young wife and two fine boys of school age, is a blue-and-white cottage towards the top of Copper Hill Street. He is a highly respected family-man—who still, *still* looks every inch a pirate.

There are a good many inches. Lean and lithe ones. Carried as if he had wet planks of a vessel swaying under his feet. Clothed, usually, in a rough dark jersey. At times the sleeves are rolled up above lavishly tattooed forearms. Weathered slacks are tucked into sea-boots. His old woolly cap is pushed back from a deeply sun-tanned, rollicking-eyed, short-bearded face of some '*old, bold mate of Henry Morgan*'. (Not so old!)

As he leaps ashore from the boat in which he's been handing out instructions to Sea-School lads on the current course, he hails you, across the strip of pebbly beach, the Prom. above it, the main street beyond, and his voice was described in Sir Walter Scott's novel of that title *The Pirate* as one that *must give the word above the storm to cut the mast and clear the deck*. (To quote this about Stan's voice may be overstating, but it's on those lines!)

Since the sea-songs collection, he is responsible for another classic; *Sailor Town*. This, I understand, is about—*Well, you know what sailors are!* However, it was published (and an American publisher is showing interest in it) later than the time when I sent out my S.O.S.—*Mayday, Mayday!* to this expert.

Instant kindly response: 'Ho! Yes! Anything I can do! "One good turn," y'know!'

(I had roughly translated for him a German shanty. He'd also asked if I'd know anything, early times, in *Greek*? 'No, good Heavens . . . but I've a friend who might—' Sir Maurice Bowra had supplied in Greek *and* English *a song for men pulling on the rope* probably the version of sea-chanty in Ancient Greece.)

After his day's work I got Stan into our sitting-room at Pomona. Long legs over the hearth-rug, smokes and drink to his hand. Smartened up, in an immaculately clean white hand-knitted pullover, dark trousers, and ultra-respectable shoes, he doesn't look any less of a sea-tough. He merely shows up what Madam Aphra Behn called *the glaring Impotence of Dress* to disguise a Personality.

You can take him anywhere (like the *White Horse* in the whisky advert!) and always he remains himself.

III

Are you a reader who is bored stiff when writers will talk shop?

Please be patient while I have one more (quite short) go at it.

Follows, the discussion between your 'romantic' feminine Story-teller and the Man of Action and Adventure (apart from his successes with pen, brush, and microphone).

'You tell me,' said this colleague, 'what's the snag in this yarn of yours.'

I gave him the story as I'd told it to my son Bill. Without interruptions, I came quickly to the point.

'As Bill said, it's not only the Captain. The ship's officers?'

'On a small boat like that there'd only be the mate. And the second mate.'

'How could he get round *them* to keep it dark?'

'Easy!—Didn't you say the Skipper was a Welshman?'

'Yes. Captain Jones.'

'Ho!' broke from Stan, *fff* ('*fump, fump, Fump!*' as the little girl at her music lesson translated the abbreviation for *fortissimo*). 'That's got it! Make 'em *all* Welsh. The three of 'em. First mate, second mate, and him. All from the same place. One o' those small villages up in the mountains. Caernarvonshire, say . . . Tryfan, some place. Been in school together. Belonging to the same Chapel. Singing the same hymn-tunes, and that. *You think a Welshman would split on another Welshman?*'

No. Oh, *no*! I ought to have remembered! Though the Welsh may fight like angry robins among themselves, they'll turn and pound to pulp any man of *another nation* who would come between the Red Dragon and his wrath with 'One of *US*.'

'If he says to keep their trap shut—Tight as wax, you bet. See what I mean?'

'Of *course*!' How could I have overlooked the *my country-right-or-wrong*, immovable, touching solidarity of the Welsh?

'That's that. Now what else have we? The crew. Got to think up something for those.' Stan drew on his pipe and paused.

Before he could speak again *I* had an idea. *Even the blind hen finds a grain* (German proverb). Or was it that a man like Stan strikes sparks out of you, when another man seems to clap a damp dish-cloth over your mouth? (Curious, by the

way, how those two different effects can be produced at
different moments by the same man.)

'Lascars!' I cried. 'Could a whole ship's crew be made up
of Lascar seamen, Stan? *They* wouldn't know . . . what *wasn't*
in the log? Mightn't have enough English—'

'Wouldn't give a damn about anything s'long as they got
their spot of hashish or whatever dope—'

That struck another spark. I'd heard about children's ayahs
—not *my* ayah—my first love!—in India.

'Supposing one drop was slipped into the baby's milk?'

'Stop him yelling at an awkward moment? That's got that!'

'It wouldn't hurt him?'

'One drop? . . . Send him off, though. Out to the world.
Out, for hours. Customs officer comes in, knows the skipper
well, seen him after every trip, knows *he's* safe enough not to
have anything aboard, ho, ho!'

Stan laughed. His eyes had the rollicking twinkle of a white
man on the Island where all kinds of strange passportless
Nationals had hob-nobbed in amicable gaiety with—I daresay
—their gaolers.

'Customs gives a casual look-round the cabin, exchanges a
couple of polite words with the skipper about Those Something
NAZIS, and off!'

'Without a glance to see what's under the towel spread
loosely over the basket of the Captain's washing!' I contributed happily.

'Never strike him. Fine! O.K. . . . Tell you another thing
might come in useful. Have him dock at Birkenhead. They
didn't have to be as particular there as they'd be at Liverpool.
Get a taxi there, waiting. They could ring up for that, y'know.
Skipper keeps that basket in his own hands—'

'Until he decants it on to his wife's lap. *That's* all I wanted!'
The situation—saved! 'Thanks a *lot.*'

'O.K. . . . At any time!' rang out the Voice that once had
joined the *seaward cheer* and shouted *midst the shouting
crew*: 'So long, now!'

The loose electric bulb above us ceased to vibrate. Stan had
gone. Back to the blue-and-white shipshape cottage in Copper

M

Hill Street. One whole wall of it was taken up by Stan Hugill's masterpiece, a canvas in oils of *The Sacking of Constantinople.* —Painted violence of destructively raging fire! Desperate battlings for life! Of slaughter, pillage and rapine! make a lurid background to the cheerfully domesticated figures of Bron and The Boys.

I got on with the disentangled rest of the Triplet-saga.

IV

None of it was any more improbable than the identity of the second of those Only Two White Men on that Island of Santa Lucia in the West Indies! I'd nearly jumped out of my chair when his fellow 'white' casually mentioned his name.

It is well-known in London's upper reaches of Letters and the Theatre. He is the top-translator of French into sensitive English prose. He once gave me an unforgettable *précis* of his own method of translation. That must have been *after* the fantastic get-together with Stan and others on the island of Santa Lucia? I know it's true. Yet—I couldn't get over it . . . Even allowing for the 'two soul-sides' of Man for the occasional uprush of the Subconscious. He, of all men! That 'Intellectual'! Highly civilised! Vulnerably reserved . . . So fastidious . . . He, of all men on earth? Lolling, probably still half-clad in sea-salted rags, under the blazing sun of the West Indies on a beach, hilariously hobnobbing and *'getting along fine'* with that mixed mob of toughs. . . .

V

My comparatively plausible yarn was finished. Published. Received fan-mail. Certain readers said it was my best yet. Not a word did I hear about inaccuracies or impossibilities.

All thanks to the touch of verisimilitude supplied by Stan Hugill—Blessings on his knowledgeable, ingenious, and imaginative pirate's-head!

Chapter Twenty
The Homesick Race

I

Sounding the speech of Home on alien beaches
Ar hyd y nos, all through the alien night,
Hear how the far Welsh echo reaches
Hearts hungry for their mountains' 'lost delight'!

Someone read this verse to me in Welsh, then (roughly) gave
me the English meaning. It was describing Welsh troops overseas during World War II. I asked for it to be repeated in
Welsh several times, so that the *rhythm* might come through in
my translation. To my shame I am not a Welsh speaker. It
seemed to me anyhow that the verse described all Welsh
people, on all alien beaches?

For of all the homesick races I think Wales tops the list.

Our second brother, who has lived for many years in Van-
couver, British Columbia, was rung up from another State of
Canada by a Voice that asked gaily,

'Do you know who is *this*?'

'I don't know who you are,' he called back, 'but I know
where you're FROM!'

Even through the long distance telephone the Voice had
held the unmistakable timbre of Home.

'Glad he sounded to hear it, too,' reported the caller from
Ottawa.

She was Lydia-the-Post-Office-Pantperthog, Merioneth, in days gone by. She is now Mrs. Jenkins. Welsh people far from their homes tend to gravitate to other expatriates. Her daughter Betti is also married to a Welshman of the noble tribe of Williams. She and her mother come for holidays, whenever possible, 'back to the Land'.

An English friend of mine declared,

'Your people aren't satisfied until they get *away* from those places with unpronounceable Welsh names. Once they *are* away from them they never stop talking about them and can't wait till they're back there !'

There's some truth in that. Naturally Welsh people know the urge to go further afield. Ambition calls. The lure of wider opportunities. Posts better paid. The chance of 'seeing a little bit of the world'. And having seen it? Admittedly they've broadened their outlook by encounters with men and cities unfamiliar. Given the sensitive, tough, observant, well-read Welshman who has also travelled and who can beat him? But where are his roots?

A song gives the answer.

At a gathering here of the British Legion in aid of soldiers' children a singer or reciter had failed to appear.

'Come on then, Mrs. Evans! *You* give us a song.'

Mrs. Evans, the small, gay, indomitable mother of growing children, pushed back her chair and got up. Unpremeditated, without accompaniment, there gushed forth one of the sweetest woman's voices to which I have ever listened in :

'I am longing for the mountains of my home.'

II

Our Vancouver-based brother wrote on November 29, 1967 —'As you know, in spite of the fact that it is 53 years since I last trod Welsh soil my memories of her hills, lakes, and rivers are as clear as ever.'

(Could any Cymro say more?)

'However, do not let us get too mushy—'

There spake the English strain, mockingly apologetic lest

too strong a hint of feeling might break through. He was thanking me for the advance copy of my book *A Trickle of Welsh Blood*.

—which arrived unsullied thanks to your superior packing.

I am delighted to have it as we are having three old friends to share my birthday dinner. I shall make sure that it lies on a conspicuous table.

I enjoyed reading it so much that, as the garden has to have daylight for winter woollies all other evening reading was ditched, and I got to the 3rd evening's reading at 12.00 midnight.

Meat and drink it is to us in 'scribble-business' when the recipient of a gift-book writes back with more than thanks and perhaps an assurance that it will 'always be treasured'. Whereas the Scribbler, toil-worn and diffident, is yearning for specific detail from the Reader. Mention of *what* (if anything) had pleased. Comment of *why* it had been disliked would be far, far preferable to no sign being given that it had even been *read*.

But here was meat and strong drink.

'The bits I particularly liked'—and this model reader enumerated several !

You mention in the Chapter '*A Smile for Autumn*' that you wonder if anybody can go back far enough to remember Tosti's *Goodbye Summer*. If you were here I could sing you the words all through to the last sob-choked cry !

He could sing.—He had been at a Choir-School. He then noted my visit to Plas Tirion . . .

This was a Caernarvonshire country-house belonging to the Rowlands family. Encircled by woods, there was, I remember —see it in a flash-back !—a rookery that speckled the sky with black wheeling dots. In the grounds there was a small lake where we had permission to skate. The inside of the house was very formal. Alarming, actually. The drawing room was a clutter of Indian things, brass trays, fringy fans . . . I had forgotten other details which my brother's letter recalled. How, from Llwyn-y-brain, our house nearly a mile away—

—we could hear the donkey, who dragged Mrs. R's chair about, letting fly with an ear-shattering bray if it was going to rain, with supporting chorus of screaming peacocks . . . It was down by the Seiont when M.U.R., R.C.R. and I were picking blackberries, that we came upon General Rowlands fishing. He had got a salmon on his line which was tangled in an over-hanging bough and I waded in and got it ashore for him. We of course looked like ragamuffins. He asked us where we lived and we told him, he said 'Good God! Are you the young Rucks?' He gave me a book on fishing which I kept for a long time, *Hoffland's British Anglers' Manual* . . .

It comes back to me, too, now the scene I missed by being at School . . . The picture of my first sister and two boys. Trampish clothes! Faces stained purple with fruit-juice. Bramble-scratched legs and hands, perfectly happy all three, blackberrying beside the Seiont . . .

General Rowlands I remember as a veteran but persistent Dandy of the Old School as he appeared every Sunday in Llanrug Church. He kept his hair and his waxed moustache a rich brown, his waist-line encased in corsets, his feet in tight patent-leather boots.

Sternly our father informed us giggle-prone children that: 'Any soldier who had won the V.C. in the Crimean War might be allowed to wear what he chose.'

There is a story about General Rowlands which I have already written down—somewhere? Never mind!—The General told this story himself, *against* himself, to another Caernarvon character. 'Captain-Tom-the-Tobacco-shop' passed it on.

Hugh Rowlands, as a very young subaltern, was about to go into action for the first time in his life.

There rushed upon him, as upon many another brave man

before and after his time, the ghastly sensation . . . *Butterflies
in the stomach*. God! A soldier and afeared? . . . Suddenly
there was a shout from the rear.

On that far-distant foreign field the voice of one of the
gipsy Lovells from Tan-y-rallt, a quite—well! non-exclusive
district of Caernarvon! called out in the vernacular the name
of a Welsh home, called out upon the Son of the House.

'Rwan yr hen Blas Tirion! rwan am biff!' (*Now then old
Plas Tirion! now for a biff!*)

Butterflies flew away and were no more.

III

À propos this book which had set those echoes sounding in my
brother's Canadian home—I thought it would be appropriate
to send a copy to the Welsh Society in Paris. Don Pryse-Jones
had belonged to this gathering. He had told me that they all
dined together on St. David's Day. It was he who gave me the
address of Madame Jean Fenestre . . . sounded inappropriately French? but perhaps she was from Brittany? Bretons
are fellow-Celts who have much of the language and the
temperament in common with the Welsh.

Madame wrote back. Full of *hiraeth* for this country,
roused by the mention of Bangor, of Bala, the Lake, the dear
small town that still spelled 'Siop' in the Welsh way. She wrote
that, whenever possible, she had taken her children, for their
holidays, *home*!

Don Pryse-Jones, now back in the States, wrote to me,

'I had pages from "Madame Fenestre" in Paris where it
[the book] seems to have enchanted the Welsh group . . . I
suppose you were misled by the name? . . .'

He gave me the story of it.

Jean Fenestre, a terribly nice person, was in England in
1939, with a family to learn English, and there met Gwendolyn Jones (Wendy for short) from Bangor. She was then
working in London. They fell in love, and then came the war
and separation. As soon as he could get to London he came
looking for her, but the house was gone, and nobody knew of

her! He then set off for Bangor to find her, but had no address there. He simply went up and down streets asking if anybody knew Wendy Jones. Naturally, Bangor was full of Wendy Joneses, and some twenty were hauled out for him . . . the whole population by this time having gotten themselves into the story, but not the right Wendy. Finally he got a trace of her, and she was sent for, and as she said,

'After this what could I do but marry the poor man, or nobody in Bangor would ever have spoken to me again.'

So she did. A happy ending . . . but still she brings the children to the hen Wlad . . .

IV

To return to the letter of the brother who is himself unlikely to return though the pull of the Old Place still holds. Even the flowers of Home have references.

He had been sent a consignment of bulbs carefully packed in a tin box. This was in years before these were dutiable and subject to restrictions. Now, in February 1968, with the Canadian garden still under snow he writes:

> The Esgair snowdrops are still wondering if it is advisable to get too far from Mother Earth. Still, Ida [his wife] manages to keep a little blossom going with winter-jasmine and forsythias . . . And are the rhododendron islands still on the pool?

This was on the upland at the top of the hill above Pantlludw, the dower-house to Esgair.

Pantlludw in the nineteen-sixties was too small to 'bed out' our three Atkin cousins. Their father had died in Australia. Their mother, *née* Ruck, brought them home to Wales. The boys, Dick, Walter, Robin, lived like young Spartans in the sturdy stone cottage at the flat top of the hill. The Lake was their bathroom. For meals they used to run down the steep woodland way to Pantlludw.

My brothers have also slept up there.

The furniture had gone. They slept on the floor on sheep-skins; slept like logs. Toil was their sleeping pill. Have men yet discovered a better one?

The Canadian letter went on :

O.L.R. and I drained it, [the Pool]. I can't remember how many years ago. (well over half-a-century.) Quite a job cleaning out years and years of accumulation of leaves, etc. Not being stream-fed, just springs, trout don't have a good spawning-ground.

I expect the whole hillside is completely changed now anyhow?

V

Changed? It is. And how!

The cottage on the hill, where our Atkin cousins spent their young boyhood and where later, my brothers sank into dream-less nights of sleep after toil stretched out on sheep-skins spread over the floor, is now like those Sicilian mountain-villages after the earthquake, ruin and rubble.

From those islands on the Pool the rhododendrons still mirror themselves in mauve and green reflections. Shimmer-ing, to break under the breeze. To re-form on the water. Sphagnum moss, goldy-green and moist still makes cushions on which the sundew spreads round red medallions.

But beyond that marge?

What has become of those wide spaces of turf open to sky and wind and the view of the Dovey Valley far, far below as it led to the distant gleam of the sea? Where—?

Gone. No more, the uplifting sight of great white clouds billowing across the skies overhead. No more the turf, threaded by tiny flat antlers of stags-horn moss is springy underfoot. All is crowded and dim under 'The Forestry'. *'Larch pricks a Cockney ear'* and Pine raises its aisles over one-seventh of the country. Larch is not even British but largely Japanese. Cheaper, growing quicker. Timber, wealth of Wales! Too much is a matter of money . . . and,

> *ah, for the fresh breeze to redden my cheeks now*
> *And lull me to sleep like a babe at the breast.*

Why quote from *The Songs of Wales*? Here is no longer the part of Wales that my brother knew. Not the Wales remembered by him and his like. . . . Better for them not to return. Might it not be like meeting again an old flame, an early love . . . ? Surprise. Incredulity. Chill where there had been thrill.

Leave it. Leave it as the enchanted distant view . . .

For—Nothing can break the Spell of Things Past!

Chapter Twenty-One
No Place Like It

I

Had you heard the Eastern proverb *To every man his home is Kashmir*? (Kashmir or Cashmere being reputedly the loveliest of all Eastern countries.)

The Welsh equivalent that I was told is even stronger. *Born in hell, it's in hell that he'd wish to live.*

Welsh people can hardly believe that anyone, in their senses, would find a word to say against Wales, once they'd been here.

I was quite shaken by the one dissentient description of our county I ever read. Here are entries from the journal of Beatrix Potter (creator of Peter Rabbit) written in 1888. She was then a young girl, so forgive her.

> May 13. Went with Mamma and Papa to Machynlleth in Merioneth. From Euston to Stafford by Holyhead Mail all very well, but the Welsh Railways are past description. Four hours to go sixty miles between Shrewsbury and Machynlleth. When mushrooms are in season the guard goes out to pick them. Machynlleth, wretched town, hardly a person could speak English.

Today, alas! it is the *minority* who carry on their conversations in Welsh.

Miss Potter gives a black to Machynlleth's hotels.

'Wynnstay Arms, to which we were directed, closed these two years. Lion, only other, a singular place.' (What did she mean by 'singular'?) Both places flourish today.

The Journal continues :

'Country most beautiful.'

Ah, she too saw it in May, loveliest of months!

This year, after a murderous Welsh winter, Spring flowers come *rushing* out in all gardens. Ferns uncurl by every stone hedge. Gorse in its first blooming spreads all hill-sides with cloth-of-gold.

In May, month of fruit-blossom, I saw that rarity the *wild* pear-tree making a storm of white in the Gwithers' grounds. It was probably self-sown, many seasons back, in congenial soil. Prized for its Spring-time beauty, its fruit is small and negligible . . . (Like some too-wonderful human romance that lacks a happy ending. What of it? Let's be thankful that there are, as Stella Gibbons once wrote, 'plenty of happy *beginnings*'.

Trees, on each side of the up-and-down road between in-and-out Dolgellau and Brithdir, fluttering brilliant young foliage, make semi-transparent veils for the slanting country-side. Higher up, vistas of mountain-land gleam in sunshine or are changefully dimmed by fleeting cloud shadows.

Further on, and below, that glint of silver is Tal-y-llyn. At the lake-side that flash of white is a nesting swan. Above, Cader Idris towers in majesty.

Truly, *country most beautiful—*

but on rather a large scale for getting about. House we went to see, Pennal Tower [*sic*] in a Wilderness. Widow, Mrs. Thruston, alarming result and warning of living in the wilds.

Village of Pennal consisted of three large chapels and about twelve other houses.

It is not so very much larger, now. 'Little and good' in fact. As for 'Widow Mrs. Thruston' of Pennal Towers, she was a family-friend of ours. Certainly slightly alarming. Not as the result of living in the wilds but because, though she was a woman of breeding and basic kindliness, sweet with children, she had a manner as brusque as a road-drill.

She told my father,

'Arthur! Your bright girl is prostituting her brains writing those silly love-stories.' Whereat Father cleared his throat of 'the Ruck mumble' and actually raised his voice in defence of his eldest child.

'*I* think Berta writes very prettily.'

('Pretty' had not then degenerated into something contemptible.)

To me, after a rollicking Christmas holidays dance at Pennal Towers, Mrs. Thruston said:

'You think everything in Life is great *fun,* don't you? It doesn't last, my girl. It's just physical. High spirits of Youth. Doesn't last after thirty.'

This didn't daunt me. As Jennie Pearl in Compton Mackenzie's novel, *The Passionate Elopement,* exclaimed:

'Thirty? What an *unnatural* age! P'raps I shan't never be thirty.' Besides, I didn't believe what Mrs. Thruston had said about it was true.

It isn't.

The Journal now has a word of praise for us.

Welsh seem a pleasant intelligent race but I should think awkward to live with.

The children exceedingly pretty, black or red, with clear complexions and bright blue eyes. The middle-aged are very plain but the old people are better.

The language is past description.

What would Plaid Cymru say to that? Guided by the agreeable voice of Mr. Gwynfor Evans it is making gallant efforts to have the *hen iaith,* the beautiful old language of Wales more universally spoken and written in its homeland.

II

Augustus John, Welsh artist and rebel, once told me that, in France, Frenchmen themselves took him for a Frenchman— 'Only for the first five minutes of my conversation,' he added truthfully. 'I couldn't keep up the perfection of my French accent for much longer.'

Admittedly Welsh people are easier with foreign languages than are the other inhabitants of Britain. Perhaps Continental trips abroad for Welsh Youth Societies will lead to their becoming *tri*-lingual?

Youth, though, is termite-minded. It takes its pleasures in groups. The gang goes sight-seeing. Together they sit at the café-tables of Italy, Switzerland, Yugoslavia and further. They are served *wine and curious meat.* They appreciate the zingier food of abroad. But if it's brought by a waiter who can understand English, and they 'would be private' they talk together in Welsh.

There was a certain waiter who had been to Cardiff, and had brought back to confront them with a single Welsh phrase: *Iech y da!* (a fact).

The young holiday-makers return to report on the trip:

'Smashing! Not one wet day the whole time we were away!'

Senior travellers relax over the first cup of good strong brown tea after the red *vino* or 'that garlicky stuff they call beer'— wherever they've been.

'Yes! we'd wonderful weather, but—Gets on your nerves after a bit, waking up to that everlasting blue sky and blazing sun—and all those crowds lying about the beaches like so much *coed bach*' (driftwood) 'and the smell of hot, hot sun-tan oil. . . . It's marvellous to be able to *breathe* again,' say they, gulping in mouthfuls of cold moist sea-mist.

Mist blots out all trace of the vaunted view except that of a strip of sodden-brown-paper-coloured sand on the near-side of the Estuary at low tide. It muffles sound.

Suddenly, a scream! Out of the sky? Phantom-like, a winged shape emerges. The seagull flaps its wings, then vanishes again like a ghost into the bone-chilling mist.

Difficult to believe there were ever warm sunny days when the quiet of the River mouth was torn to shreds by the racket of imported speed-boats!

For where is now the tourist-traffic? The line of cars halted at the kerb all the way from the Church Hall to the station? Closed cars, many of them with occupants who sat reading the paper. Or just sat. Where are the young parent-visitors who made 'the Prom' into the Pram-walk? Where, the traffic-jams of the swingier young along the narrow age-cracked pavements outside the row of shops, scanning the display-windows of D. O. Hughes, Drapers, announcing in authoritative Midland accents, 'I quite *like* that stripey job!' Wearing near-Costa Brava mini-clothes, novel hair-colours that look, to aboriginals such as ourselves, as if they were staging some fantastic masquerade, where are they? What has become of an alien population that came flocking to 'this picturesque resort' for the golf-links, the beach, the yachting, trips up to the Bearded Lake, and through the Happy Valley?

Gone. Trailing their caravans, with baggage or a canoe topping their cars they're off until next holiday season.

A village resumes its character.

Familiar figures, head-scarved, rain-coated, carrying shopping-bags, stop. 'Good-morning. *Not* a very good morning, is it? No, indeed.' Disappear.

The big green Crossville 'bus from Towyn lurches into sight. One passenger climbs out, tells you that it's not a *very* good morning. The 'bus waits at the big lettered BUS STOP on the wet asphalt near the entrance to the Church.

'Colder today it's gone,' said the departing passenger. 'Feels like more rain, too.'

It feels as if it never had been May.

Gay, shrill chatter, light running footsteps burst through the mist. Children are hurrying home from school to dinner.

The green 'bus waits . . . Nobody to get in? It restarts with a jerk like a sleeper awakening, and goes on. Empty.

Dear old Aberdovey, like scores of Abers and Llans all over the Principality, is itself again after an invasion. In shops they tell you it's gone very quiet, now. Still! Nice and peaceful! More like home.

Yes. No place like it.

Chapter Twenty-Two
The Magic Casement

I

'The prestige that once came from having one's *name in print* or *on a book-jacket* gave place to the prestige of being *heard on the radio,*' said Kenneth Harris to me last time I met that well-known personality. 'Now that prestige has gone to having *been on the Telly.*—I know my *Observer* articles I wrote were the best things I'd done,' he told me (a bit sadly). 'Not a word about them from the engineers in the studio, ever. But now it's "*Saw* you last night, Mr. Harris! You WERE good!" '

How do you regard television? As just a *bar* to pleasant sociable conversation?

Some see it as the Top Evil Influence of our Time. Bringing, into the home, scene of Violence-in-Action, Killing Glorified, Sex-in-Squalor, etc., etc.

Others hail it as the Modern Miracle that has transformed millions of lives that seemed uneventful, restricted, drab, by giving them the entry into What's Going On in the wider, more exciting world outside.

To house-bound, bedridden yearners for shows, Theatres, and the Ballet now impossibly out-of-reach, that magic invention has brought stage, and drama and players as visitors into their very rooms, to be watched in comfort.

N

II

To me television has meant pleasant outings 'With pay'.

Aled Vaughan of the Welsh B.B.C. had now moved from Swansea to Cardiff. Here he was working in the T.V. Studios. He asked me, rather dubiously, whether I thought I could manage with 'a medium so new to me'. I said I would like to be given the chance to try it. (Everything once, anyhow.)

I took the long train-journey, was met, accommodation for the night had been arranged.

The studio of the new medium was, compared with sound-radio studios, a scene of Chaos and Old Night. It seemed high as a Cathedral. A place of unexpected bright lights alternating with deep shadow. Through which moved shapes of men busied with shapes of unfamiliar machinery—Well, in any case all machinery is unfamiliar to me. Fool that I am I have never learnt to use a sewing-machine or a typewriter, let alone drive a car (whereby, no doubt, fatality has been avoided). The floor, as I saw from the entrance, would be baffling. A labyrinth of wrist-thick serpenting cables. They looked like so many lurking cobras. Ready at any moment to raise evil heads, strike, wind themselves about an ankle, trip up the newcomer.

So I stood perfectly still, as I have done at a crowded London street-crossing, and held out my hand. People respond kindly to this gesture. My hand was at once taken into a firm reassuring male grasp. One of those half-seen shapes guided and set me down in a chair. Old Night surrounded me, except for a light, blank panel that confronted me and the narrow shaft of brilliance that stabbed my face.

Aled's voice out of the gloom instructed me, 'Look straight at Mr. Cliff Michelmore, Berta, won't you, when he speaks?'

'Yes; oh yes—'

I knew I was to be interrogated about my book just published. Cliff Michelmore was a well-known interviewer—'*A dear fellow*' was the verdict on him by my London friends

Antony Thorne and his wife. I prepared to look straight at the dear fellow. One of the few maxims of early childhood that I have found *right,* and have retained is: '*Always to look straight at whoever is speaking to you.*' But where was he?

Out of that blank panel a discarnate voice said pleasantly, 'Good evening, Miss Ruck.'

Wouldn't anyone have found it a bit unnerving?

I hadn't realised that Cliff Michelmore in London was to speak to me in Cardiff like Jove out of a cloud, but I pulled myself together to return the aerial greeting.

He went on,

'Tell me, why did you call your book *A Smile for the Past*?'

'Oh, because—'

This had been the covering title of a series of short broadcasts I'd done with Aled at Swansea about celebrities I'd met and shows I'd seen in my Victorian and Edwardian days. So I was advised to use it for the longer book they made. I was just going to say so, for this interview, but suddenly I found myself ditching that and saying, instead, what was also perfectly true but impromptu, unintentional, and the sort of thing of which Welsh people say it was *given* to me.

'I called it that because there are only two ways of looking at The Past. With tears—or with a smile. And I think a smile is best?'

Mr. Cliff Michelmore seemed to think so too. I felt that something sympathetic hid behind that 'blank dark canvas' of a screen. I actually forget what the other questions were. I did my best with them, but nothing else was 'given' to me and I felt I ought to have been better.

'Aled, I'm sorry. I'm afraid I wasn't very good.'

'We'll ask London.'

One of the anonymous Shapes emerged from Outer Darkness and announced:

'London's very happy.'

So then I was happier.

III

Everything once, I'd thought, about screen-appearance. But there were to be several times.

I have even had the honour and glory of having an entire film-unit down at Aberdovey to take pictures and talk to me in the place where I lived. Make a noise like a Novelist at Home?

I'd a hunch this wouldn't be as much fun as the 'outings'. Apart from the disturbance and disruption of daily life it would mean to my husband.

He was a confirmed Anti-Listener. 'That Box' was his name for a radio-set. Impossible to convey the scornful distaste he put into the phrase. Another was *Tinned Music*. Yet he never failed to turn on the programme from King's College Chapel, Cambridge, and to listen enthralled to every note. To that, and to the News, he gave access.

As for T.V. he wasn't even an Anti-Viewer.

He'd never 'viewed'—Even the outside of That Box.

He would have felt differently, I know, had he lived to see it evolve into the magic casement that gives us at first-hand and close the sight and movement of wild life. Great Cats of the Nature Reserve take the pose of our fireside kitten as they relax in African sunshine. Giant Turtles basking on Darwin's remote island, nosing the hand of the investigating stranger, tame because still ignorant of Man. Dolphins at under-sea play, gliding, curvetting. . . . One loses the sense of being indoors, earth-bound, as one watches the dolphins dive.

Certain human beings have, by dedicated training, attained the effortless grace of animals. These, too, visit us by T.V. For us, cooped between walls, a Spectre leaps free from a great semi-transparent up-surge of spray to turn into a water-skier.

Swift as a kingfisher's flash-past come to us the Dancers-on-Ice. In mid-career he swings his light-limbed partner off her feet. Lifts her high in arm. Lets her down softly as a falling leaf drifts to the ice. Enlaced and smiling, they whirl in their waltz all round the arena. Slow to a halt. He bows, she curtsies low. . . . They are going—Oh, stay! 'Again!' as a small boy I know called to a peacock he saw for the first time spread his coloured feather-wheel then furl it to a trailing tail. 'Again!' No. Faded, the sight of beauty from our eyes.

My husband as an unbribe-able artist would have known better than many viewers how to appreciate this revelation by magic casement. Even so, I can imagine a reference made to Sir John Falstaff's tavern-account and its 'intolerable' proportion of sack to bread! the other way about if it came to how much ugly rubbish you must view before there was vouchsafed to you the Glimpses . . .

Àpropos taverns, what excitement at the Dovey Hotel where Mr. Aled Vaughan and Mr. John Morgan had put up for the night! The rest of the unit drove over next morning. They reminded me of the camera crew I'd watched working on the filming of *Autumn Crocus* long ago in the Tirol. Same cheerful O.K.—Bert? industrious type. One of the young men with them didn't seem to belong, somehow. . . . He looked . . . different. Lazily amused, more . . .

I'd told my husband that Maudie, my youngest sister, would come in to lunch with him.

'I don't know where I shall be all day . . . They're going to do things near the Roman Rocks. Or the Sea School perhaps. They won't be coming near you. I promise. I've got to go now—'

'You carry on.'

I was *carried* on.

It was at the time when I still went into the sea summer and winter, and the B.B.C. people had heard of this, asked if it were true.

'But you didn't go in *this* morning? *With this wind?*'

'It was rather windy. A wave knocked me over, actually.'

'Gee, she must be tough!'

I'm not sure that they believed me. Aled did. But he wasn't going to send me in again.

'I want her coming down *here*. On to the beach.'

It was not a part of the beach that I usually do go down. Getting on towards what used to be the old Blacksmith's Forge of my early childhood. However, the thing was to get the outdoor background right for a picture.

There were spectators.

There were takes and retakes until everybody—not only I —was extremely hungry....

After the lunch-break came the shooting of the indoor pictures...

Goodness!

Let me sit back and remember them.

We lived then at Pomona on what was known to a French visitor as Le Boulevard Maritime, a pale Victorian terrace. Bordered by 'comic strips' of garden, wallflowers, hydrangea, railed in as if against jewel-robbery, with slate steps up to front doors. Facing the wall to the beach, the mouth of the Estuary. High as a lighthouse, with stairs and stairs up to my room.

I had a big room. I needed it. It was my working-room, my bedroom, the place where I kept my books, photographs and belongings. It was also known, during the war, as Auntie Berta's coffee-stall, for here was where my small near-grandson Niki brought young friends for light refreshments. I had an electric kettle, and a *cache* in a sizeable old black sea-chest. The room had a big three-sided window far above road, beach-wall, beach, bathing-huts, mouth of Estuary, Bar, to that incomparable sea-view....

But the view, that afternoon, of the room itself!

The T.V. unit had, in an incredibly short time, made an expert scene-shifting job of it.

Everything was somewhere else. Including my desk. My private-property *desk,* if you please, that nobody was supposed to touch. Even the near-grandson had been told off on an occasion when he'd cast down on it his 'repulsive damp fishing-tackle'—You can't tell off the T.V. though. I know, now, how a man feels when he comes home to find spring-cleaning going on in his own familiar corner. . . . The noise they must have made moving that heavy sea-chest—! Books had been pulled out. My wardrobe, fortunately, was permanently outside on the landing. But where was my *bed*?

Pushed to the side where the sea-chest had always lived. On the bed lay the young man who'd seemed different from the rest of the unit. Comfortably relaxed. Reading my *Paris Match*.

An echo came to me of an ancient music-hall ditty:

> *When I found her cousin Fred*
> *With his boots on in my bed,*
> *Well, I had to tell the girl she didn't suit.*

This Reclining Figure couldn't be a trainee for the film-industry? Possibly a journalist with V.I.P. connections and *carte blanche* to go Anywhere.

Not so my sister and my landlady Miss Zoë Williams. They in their innocence had imagined they could be let in as sports-spectators. They had been put in their place, and now camped on the stairs outside the shut door.

I saw where I was put to sit and answer questions.

Where born? India? *Not* Wales. Had I always lived here? Methods of work? How many hours a day? etc. How many novels had I written? One a year?

I said, as I've said to any interviewer who cared to ask, that I knew that only because my first novel was published in 1913. That was the date of my younger son's birth. I was finishing a chapter just before he signalled his arrival. It had been a toss-up between the boy and the book. The boy won.

'Are you writing another book now, Miss Ruck?'

'Always.'

'Do any of your family write or paint? *Not* either of your sons?'

I told how the elder one as a very small boy had asked me in a crowded 'bus, 'What is ART?' and I, embarrassed and petulant, had said firmly, 'Nothing you'll ever have anything to do with, I hope.' To which he'd returned, 'Then why is Art in Heaven?'

'And about your husband and *his* work—?'

'I'm afraid I can't answer for him.' I could only wonder what he was going to say about the furniture removal activities that had gone on over his head.

I was feeling tired at last. If I had been able to see what they had done with my looking-glass it would have shown me a woman who, instead of looking, as kind people said, years less than her age, was that day expecting the traditional telegram from the Queen congratulating her subject on her hundredth birthday.

'And what should *you* say, Miss Ruck, was your recipe for a Happy Old Age?'

This was the *End*.

I answered forthright.

'There isn't one. Old Age is hell!' adding hastily, 'Here, don't put *that* in!'

The lounger on my bed lifted his head from my *Paris Match* and, in what used to be called an 'Oxford' voice, called out 'Oh, but yes! Have that in. That's *good*.'

They had it in.

I heard this later from one of our cousins in London. 'I casually turned on our set to see what was on, and there was *Berta*! Saying out loud that Old Age was HELL!'

'They've finished now,' I told my husband, soothingly. 'They're *just* going.'

He looked up from *The Times* crossword.

'Aren't any of them coming in to see me?' Perfectly mild he sounded. Not a word about the bumps and thumps over his head, the tramplings up and down the stairs outside.

'I—We didn't think you'd want to be bothered.'

'Surely I'm to be allowed to meet one of them for five minutes?'

I brought in Aled. He sat down opposite O.O.'s armchair, had a cigarette and a chat. He came out in ten minutes. I heard he'd reported to the others that Oliver Onions was a Nice Quiet Old Gentleman who didn't seem to mind the noise.

Men are like children: you haven't a hope of predicting what effect they'll choose to make on strangers.

I, who'd married Four Men at Once—as any woman has done whose husband is a genius—had not encountered the Nice Quiet Old Gentleman.

So I suppose there were Five Men?

IV

My next T.V. sortie was to Cardiff again. Cobra-strewn floor; the Cathedral-high ceiling. Mysterious mechanisms, anonymous ministrants moving about them as before. This time I was not required to look straight at and speak to a blank panel that was Mr. Cliff Michelmore in London. More difficult! I was to sit in the surround of Chaos and Old Night with a shaft of brilliance on my face and to hold converse with a whole group of barely-glimpsed Entities who were to be placed in the murk of a shaded background. . . . It was to be *Live*— That is, no script made.

Aled gave me a swift run-through. He issued instructions.

'Drop your hand, then. . . . Not you! Wait till Colin drops *his* hand, Berta. Then start.'

Plaintive protest from me:

'I can't see Colin (whoever he is) let alone his hand!'

'Stand a bit nearer her,' says Aled, patiently.

I had a sudden realisation of the gruelling many-faceted job of work meant by the making of a T.V. drama, with full cast, several locations, the costumes as well as the *words* of perhaps six players to consider . . . I'd never really thought of the organising—had you? Has anyone, except those actually involved?

Even with just me the problem had been raised—

'What is she to WEAR?'

Specially for this occasion I had put on my Glitter Coat. It's based on the lovely wide-sleeved brocade Eastern jacket brought me from India by my brother many years ago. When I'd worn it almost to fringy shreds, a kind and expert friend had taken the pattern and made for me an exact copy in black-and-gold lamé . . . Everybody had liked it, everywhere I'd worn it . . .

Except here.

'That'll never do,' pronounced some stranger, and everybody with him agreed that it would 'dazzle' on the screen. You wouldn't *see* anything but dazzle.

'Take it off, dear, d'you mind?'

'Not at all.' Ours is the Adaptable Sex. Today I was the Puppet in the hands of Professionals. Off came the Glittercoat. It was reft from me, disappeared into outer darkness.

'What's she got on under that?'

I'd have thought my plain black frock was quite inoffensive.

'No. Oh, definitely not. It's the same shade as that hair, man. Can't have all that black. Had she a light coat?'

'I'm afraid not.'

'Black, too? Gosh. Better send for the wardrobe mistress.'

Enter wardrobe mistress, a grave young creature taking herself and her job very seriously. As, of course, she should. Over her arm she carried a selection of draperies. One after another was swathed about the Puppet. Finally the Professionals settled for a neutral-coloured sort of stole. Wardrobe mistress arranged it on me. In real life I wouldn't have been found drowned in it! (Yes: I have a trickle of Irish blood as well, but what of it?) Actually it 'harmonised all right for the screen'. That I did not do too badly in the programme was thanks to Aled, who quite unexpectedly started before Colin's drop of the hand by bringing me a sizeable mug of orange-juice. I sipped.

'Aled! There's *gin* in this. I never drink g—'

'You drink it.'

I drank, and, surprisingly! it was as rain on a parched plant.

Our Welsh-speaking brother sent me a cutting, with his translation, from a Welsh newspaper. According to this I seem to have been not unpleasing to the house. Though I do, a little, regret not having had on the Glitter Coat.

V

The next T.V. session in which I was invited to join was after I moved camp, alone, from Pomona.

I now live in a place up the hill above the Church. Its three-storied, sharply-gabled, stucco-masked Victorian façade is less than decorative, but oh, blessings on the inside space! on the freedom from all seaside-holiday immigrant-din! Late-Victorians built for privacy, surrounded by 'grounds'. So here a high screen of ilex shades the lawns and shuts out all sight of the square Church tower, roofs, road, and crowds below. Beyond, one sees lots of sky, sands, and Bay. This house, Bryn Tegwel, was once the home of a golfing, Bridge-playing, old bachelor Eton master (retired). He left it to Eton. Apparently Eton recoiled. I am glad. For it is now run as a Nursing Home —in which I am not a patient but rather as it were a lodger in a pleasant Hotel where I can write, have friends, come in and go out as I like.

That morning, through the wide entrance, past the ever-open iron-work gates and into the gravelled approach (which could form the site for at least three of The New-Way-of-Life bungalows) 'the T.V.' arrived. On the dot. As arranged. 8 a.m. The earliest yet for a broadcast. I am earlier, and was ready. In some neighbourhoods visits by 'the T.V.' are no more of a rarity than the man coming to look at the gas-meter? Here, the staff had been pleasurably excited ever since the date was announced. I was to make one in a programme *Augustus John, the Man as I knew him.* The note told me that I should be asked about this great Welsh artist's saying that he envied me for possessing the strain of authentic gipsy blood while he, John, could not lay claim to a drop of it. Though, goodness knows, he *looked* pure Romany, he spoke their language, was asked to join in all their 'things', and he certainly dressed the part.

My first idea for this film was a bit of a gipsy make-up for myself. Red shawl perhaps? sackcloth apron, men's boots, basket of clothes-pegs, and the 'P.R.' as my sisters call That Hat, Past Repair! but still *rather* picturesquely gipsy? On second thoughts No. Too mountebank. Better be just ordinary; only those earrings.

The first of the visitors was announced: Mr. Ned Kelly. 'Your interviewer.'

A smiling and courteous young Irishman.

'Now, Miss Ruck, if you don't mind? We'll run over what we'd like you to say . . . then we can switch on to all those *busy* eavesdroppers—'

'How many are you?'

A moment later my room seemed full to bulging with that bunch of agreeable young Welshmen. Politely they asked if they might move a few things out? 'We will *replace* everything, Miss Ruck!' they promised. Meanwhile they crowded my room with T.V. equipment brought by them in the two large cars now parked in the Approach. They conferred together where to put *me*. So illustrative of the New Way of Life that apparently they answered only to the names of the implements *Light—Camera—Sound* with which they wrought.

'Will you sit at your desk, Miss Ruck, please?'

'If I *can*.' Gadgets to right of me, cobras to left of me—

'Never mind . . . Sit her the other side. It won't show.'

I sat, feeling as if I had lost my way in an old Marine Stores or other junk dump.

'Ready, Sound? . . . Light!'

Piercing brilliance shafted into my eyes. Then we got on with it. It was all familiar enough now.

Except that they were all so unusually *formal*. Exquisitely polite! New brooms? It was a newly formed Company: Harlech. I hadn't seen one of them before.

The Interviewer:

'I *should* like that bit you wrote somewhere—Description of Augustus John lolling on a beach in France . . . Like a sunburnt merman with those lovely little naked babies sprawling all over him. Could you remember it, Miss Ruck?'

'Oh, yes.'

'Now, if you would take this book, then put it down on the desk, and turn your head a little to me, as if you were just going to speak—Would you?'

It didn't seem much of a feat?

But I heard one of them murmur approvingly: *'Natural!'* The next moment they were packing up, no more than a moment after that, it seemed, the room was clear of paraphernalia. And my things, even my books! were where they belong.

'If you are ever out of a job,' I said, 'you'd get one at once in a first-class furniture removal firm.'

The young proprietors of Bryn Tegwel invited the 'working-party' to adjourn to their top-flat for coffee break and a chat. The Interviewer talked of time he'd spent in the States; he hadn't cared for New York when he was there—'All Muggers and Truman Capote!' There were other things, but he obviously preferred *here*. (Always a good mark for this from the Welsh.)

The whole staff, I think, had contrived to get a look-see at the T.V. unit.

Where all were liked, the one called 'Sound' appeared to have been first favourite, though he was not heard to contribute one word beyond 'Thank you and Goodbye.'

Then away down the hill and off to Bala, Blaenau-Ffestiniog or wherever duty called sped the two big car-loads of equipment and cheerful young men. Their next date was with some full-blooded gipsies who had known Augustus John.

Everybody was loth to see them go.

'Well, we shall all see the picture early next month.'

Frustration.

The unforeseen strike by I.T.V. technicians killed all 'early next month' hopes.

'It *may* only be postponed until later,' I told would-be viewers who had turned on me, as if it were my fault. 'Anyway they have honourably *paid* me, and it was fun having the unit here, wasn't it?'

'But we'd wanted to see what they'd *done*! When shall we, d'you think?'

A play isn't on till the curtain goes up ! You'll know when a film is coming on the air by seeing the name of it on the screen. *That's Show-business!*

(In fact it was only a *few* days later than promised that the film did appear.)

VI

My favourite flash-back among T.V. memories reads like *The Tale of the Three Bears*. But it's true.

I met these three little boys trotting down the road from Penhelig Terrace towards the turning into Nantiesin. They halted in front of me. Looked up. I thought they were going to ask if I could tell them the time, please ?

The biggest of the small boys, who might have been eight years old, said confidently,

'I *saw* you on telly-vision.'

The next small boy said,

'*I* saw you, too.'

The smallest of the three piped up,

'Did you see Us ?'

Chapter Twenty-Three
They are now
the Grown-Ups

This chapter was to have been headed: '*We* are now the Grown-Ups.'

That was what one of us said on the day that Father, the last of our Grown-Ups, left us to it thirty years ago.

Some of us felt oddly doubtful about it. We had, ourselves, realised that the Victorian and Edwardian park-palings of Convention and Tradition were not the immovable barriers our Grown-Ups believed in. But we believed in keeping park-palings, if of a wider set kind, perhaps, about the Young . . . *some* of the conventions, the *better* traditions . . . We had to pass those on. We were the Grown-Ups—weren't we?

On second thoughts, no.

Thirty years or more ago this may have been true. Not now. You ask 'How come?'

On the strongest-yet blast of the Wind of Change.

Please, 'Look on this picture and on that.'

Picture One: MATING IN THE STONE-AGE.

Heavy mountain-mist over bleak hill-side strewn with boulders of Cambrian rock.

Cave-man, clad in skin of pre-historic beast, dragging captured and screaming female of the species by the hair, off to his lair.

Picture Two: COURTSHIP ('Nice People' called it COMING OUT) in the LATE VICTORIAN ERA.

Brilliant ball-room.

Personable bachelor, impeccable tails and white tie, glancing towards group of chaperone-guarded debutantes.

Prettiest deb. silently palpitates *Will he ask me?* . . . *Last night he did say 'Miss Sybil, may I drop the "Miss"?' Won't he . . . Oh! He's making straight for the girl with those pearls . . . Her horrid father owns a whole railway-line, so of course. . . .*

Band strikes up selection from *The Catch of the Season.* Young man approaches :

'My dance, I *think*, Sybil ?'

She rises sedately, evading his look.

He mutters into the music,

'I happen to love you, didn't you know?'

The contrast between the Stone-ager hauling his mate by the hair to his cave (*so different from the home-life of our dear Queen* as the old Victorian lady said after being taken to a production of *Antony and Cleopatra*)—that contrast is not so very much wider than the gap between the Nineteenth Century scene—and Now.

In every way !

Governments have crashed, laws reversed, communications giddily speeded up by air travel, space-travel taken for granted as the next method, so are inventions vast alike for Civilisation or Destructions. Science running rampant through Education.

'Ah, *but*—'

Are you one of those who will protest with your last gasp *'Human Nature doesn't change!'*

Do you then make no allowance for the way *circumstances* so basic may have altered it? Draughts of the forbidden making up for the memory of banked-down rebellion?

This is the Age of Permissiveness, Pop, and the 'New Rock' that has rocked the Nature of Ex-Grown-ups to the marrow of the bones.

Lately I got a letter from a friend of mine Overseas, who was a Grown-up of my own era, though she is younger than I am. I know her to be a most kind-hearted, charming, intelligent woman, experienced—but of her experience of the

Nature, Manners and Customs of the Now Generation she writes :

> I have got along quite well in and have many nice friends there, but on the whole they are a brash, sexy, and lawless people, the young people are *so rude* and mostly *run the home* . . . the parents seem *afraid* of them. . . . At one of the *better* Universities the latest thing is that they (the students) want is for *them* to pick the Professors and get rid of those they don't like, also they want to do away with examinations,

(This, I admit, rings a bell ringing distantly from my school-days at Saint Winifred's, Bangor, not U.S.A., but Wales.)

> and, get *this,* Berta ! they want a *pub* on the *campus* so that they can drink Beer between classes ! so they have taken over the University, locked the Professors out until their demands are met. So this will give you some idea of what a Godless, lawless young set we have. The trouble is we have no one in power with any guts. Why don't they call out the Army and force them out, and then close the University and tell them when they come there to *learn* (which the University is for) and to act like ladies and gentlemen they can come back but *not before*. But all those in the Government seem to be afraid of them. It's a pretty sad state of affairs . . . (end quote)

This seems to me to express extreme measures on both sides?

More on the moderate side is the view of another friend, of my own trickle of Welsh blood, but living at present on the other side. Offa's Dyke. To him I had reported the case of a mutual friend. This friend's only son had been brought up from earliest childhood in the traditions of the heir to an ancient country-estate, now enlarged and prospering. An historic and beautiful house rich in family portraits and heirlooms. And, not least, a proud old name, which with the traditions, was to be carried on in perpetuity.

o

Scarcely had the lad reached his twenty-one than he announced his wish to break with Tradition, to leave home and the plans for continuity and to launch out on lines of his own . . .

I wrote, appalled at this, knowing what it must mean on both sides, but feeling sure some compromise would be effected?

The reply from my friends—(quote)

We were surprised, but less so on second thoughts . . . not so unlike what we see happen around us with and by many of the young here. The discipline of the previous generations, which would not have allowed it to happen, being removed inevitably makes these traumas more common.

It must be hell in different ways for parents. I suppose it is a close relation of the problems of Chicago and the Pope in a detached facet. (End quote)

There was the feeling for what restrictions can do to the growing-up Young.

It's not by forbidding the Wine that you make the Total Abstainer.

I wrote this just after the big student-demonstration in London, by Anti-Vietnam War marchers and others. Bloodstained Revolution—Police and Press were prepared for it. They were revved up for Armageddon.

The Expected did not occur—to anything like the anticipated extent.

This I had from the horse's mouth. The horse (my granddaughter on T.V. London) paid a flying visit to me in Wales the following weekend. I had been anxious about her.

She admitted that she and her camera-crew had been kept 'terribly anxious'—Oh, about the expensive new Japanese electronic camera equipment. Might have got damaged in the jostle of the crowds. It was O.K., though but for a few incidents. As for the students. A lot of them ended up by linking arms and singing *Auld Lang Syne*. 'We got shots of that . . .'

I feel like organising a Petition of Anti-Half-a-Million Pounds-payers. Was that the bill for extra Police expenses and built-up windows? Cheaper first to have listened to student-grievances and to have redressed those found justifiable?

And what about the definite *ex*-Grown-up Generations? What is the attitude apropos ourselves in The Now?

Being Ex—

Would this mean that our fate is to be treated (with luck) as Cherished fossils? Or (without luck) as Beings of Nuisance-Value Only? Or, even, Oldies-to-be Ignored?

Look on the Bright Side! I sometimes suspect the Current Young have more thought for the Current Old than we had.

I can't be the only one of the family who remembers our Mother declaiming more than once, and so dramatically!

'All you children *care* about is the PURSUIT of PLEASURE !'

We laughed; then. But wasn't there some truth in it?

When I was an Art-Student at the Slade, what *did* we 'care about', apart from our drawing? Getting into our special cliques for outings. Or dances. Or arranging parties to go and giggle at melodramas like *The Worst Woman in London* at the Old Surrey Theatre. We never gave a thought to people who were past those things . . . whereas—

Our descendants join a Society well-named *The Samaritans* . . . Would we, at their age, have devoted any of our spare-time to taking Old Age Pensioners out for little walks in Regent's Park or along the Spaniards Road? There were no Old Age Pensioners in our Day. There was plenty of Old Age. We did nothing about it. Did we dream of discussing with our Grown-Ups how factory-conditions might be altered, or— face it! We and our Grown-Ups, whatever we were like in family life, had less social conscience than some of these teen-agers who come in for such abuse.

One heartening trend in our disrupted epoch is that a number of the live and current Young do evince a wish to join groups to Do Something for Those now of antique-value only —if that. Mr. Selwyn Lloyd has instituted a base-Headquarters office for these volunteers. All over the provinces, too, they spread.

They visit the Housebound! Bring them their tea. Do their shopping. Remember to post their letters—having even procured the extortionate and resented stamps to put on them. Keep them in contact with the Outside Now by chat of their own unfamiliar activities. Their winter bird-watching in the Orkneys when their mini-car was the only sleeping accommodation and even their hot-water bottle froze solid by the morning. Their cross-Asian motor-venture. Some lads have raked in their boon-companions, on off-days, and all of them have got busy with painting and papering their houses. Let these examples of real warm-heartedness cancel out their— what *our* Grown-ups would have called—Bad Manners. Their failure to answer letters by return of post (or even to answer). Their lack of small graceful superfluous apologies? or of thanks?

Do we demand too much when we want *their* better social conscience *added* to the best things Our Grown-Ups thought essential? Why can't we have BOTH?

> *Why must we 'neath the leaves of coronal*
> *Put any kiss of pardon on their brow?*

to misquote. Much they'd care about our pardon. (I bet few of the young have a clue where that came from.)

In a grey mood I went *on* with that deplorable Has-Been Habit of Dragging in obsolete quotations. This gives the Mods, I thought—This clinches the situation—

> *The things we think are proper they wouldn't*
> *thank us to give,*
> *And the things we know are rotten they say are*
> *the way to live—*

and never sending so much as a post-card—This was when a letter arrived from one of them. The writer was the young career-woman who seemed to give something of a coronal to the Old Hand—I mean Head. It was written to acknowledge the strivings of an aged relative to cheer the career-chit in question during a (to her) important new feature of her daily toil on television.

It was a job a good deal more exacting even if considerably better paid than anything the ancestress had achieved in her more leisurely girlhood (circa 1907 ?)

With a shock of pleasure she read (quote) :

Thank you very very much for the stream of letters and post-cards during the making of [name of first film which she das directing.]

Can't tell you how much new strength it gave me to have words of cheer and encouragement to read on the way to yet another day of fear and trembling.

Though it can't be written on it, the [name of film occupation] is dedicated to you [Ends quote]

So, this time I'll let the trick be taken by one of the Young or Current Grown-Ups.

Chapter Twenty-Four
'That's for Remembrance'

I

Shortly, it will be November again. Remembrance Day. Poppies on all cars, in all coats. Jars of chrysanthemums, with paper notes of loving messages written by those who are 'left to grow old', placed on the two stone panels on which are printed the names of those from this village who fell in the two World Wars.

(There is just room for these. One prays that there need be no others.)

Veterans of those wars; groups of the two sections of the British Legion will line up, and the little girls who serve as Brownies and the older girls from Rhowniar who are doing an Outward Bound Sea School course. The lads have their own chapel. All is curiously homelike. I think there can be no Aberdovians who do not know, or do not know all about the other Aberdovians gathered about this stretch of road between the Church wall and the familiar sight of the old Estuary dear, whether under misty rain or a 'bright interval' of November sunshine. That is where we have the advantage over the great crowds who gather in Whitehall and who will see the Queen herself lay the wreath at the foot of the dominant Cenotaph. We shall watch our own Standard-bearer (Betty Williams, who at seventeen years of age joined up with her brother) stand with her colleague of the Men's Section of the British Legion and slowly, in the perfect timing which has won competitions, lower the standards in salute to the local *lads who will never grow old*, the fallen in two World Wars. Our Vicar, in his surplice, and the Nonconformist Ministers will stand together in a brotherly friendliness (which would hardly have been seen in my childhood) to read the Service in alternate English and Welsh. There will be the customary placing of poppy-wreaths, the customary momentary pauses, standings to attention, salutes, quick right-about turns. The Two Minutes Silence. The same ritual is followed at the same time all over the Kingdom. Over many other lands.

To me the most moving part of the Service is when our Vicar, in the clear diction of the Welsh voice which gives recognition to every uttered syllable, reads aloud the names written on the stone.

II

'This means Christian names to all of us,' as a soldier of the 1918 war said to me of the Cenotaph just after it was unveiled.

Those names would run into the thousands.

These make a comparatively very short list but each name evokes remembrance. Pride, Affection as well as Grief.

Laurence Ruck—named amongst those from the memorial-stone. My first cousin. So fond of 'mucking about with boats'. Often, he took over the old ferry-boat from his constant pal, Edda Bell. Laurence, with countless others, was an only son.

Max Laddie—from the Commandos. These gave, in their time here, a Foreign Legion touch of gaiety, the exotic, and romance. He married the hostess of his billet and left a lovely baby called Patricia. I've a flashback of him at the local Concert, dancing with tireless verve and expertise, a solo Schuh-plättler. This, after he'd just come off a thirty-mile exercise march.

John Rees—the Vicar read out. That was the name, following the Flt/Lt. R.A.F. in clear black letters on the sand-

coloured stone. His name as a flyer. His full name as a writer
is John Llewelyn Rhys.

III

Have you read his novels? *The Flying Shadow, England is
my Village, The World Owes me a Living* and the others? If
not you have so far missed the best short stories ever written,
or, probably ever to be written about flying.

He had cherished two ambitions. His wife, Helen Rhys
(nom-de-plume Jane Oliver) tells of these in her illuminating
preface to his *England is my Village.* 'He wanted to fly and
he wanted to write, and he did both.' How brilliantly! In how
few and succinct sentences he gives the whole 'feel' of flight.
Exaltation, tension, fatalism, nearness of death, triumph. In
one story *Return to Life* he has it all. He puts across—No!—
He *puts the reader* into what he writes. You are with it all,
you listen to the flying instructor. With the glass placed where
he can watch his pupil's face, you *see* the light mist 'as the
bloom on a plum, that makes one rub one's goggles with the
back of one's glove', or 'the shadow of the aircraft curving on
a cloud', you *share* the company of pilots on a test-flight, or
taking off for a raid, glancing down at the coast-line and
thinking 'this is the edge of England . . .' returning . . .

I have had the privilege of meeting John Llewelyn Rhys
and the wife who shared so wonderfully both his lives. Curiously, those flash-backs seem to merge into those *read.* I can
hardly distinguish being put, at a party, beside that pleasantly-
mannered young countryman of mine who greeted me with
the friendly phrase,

'Have a drop of beer, Miss Ruck,' from sitting for eight
hours in the raiding aircraft next that (fictional?) young
Canadian who was 'all excitement and relief' upon landing,
meeting questions of pals.

One *hears* the terser British exchange, the

'Were there many fighters up?'

'We got there.'

'. . . Any luck?'

'Yes. As far as I could see we blew the place to hell.'

'And fighters?'

'Not so hot . . . But one of them got a lucky shot in.'

'Jimmy?'

'Yes.'

You are with them as they go into the Mess. The Thursday party in full swing. Entertainers. A terrific row going on. (You *hear* it!)

The entertainer who is a pianist (and rather drunk) begins to play a song about hanging up the washing on the Siegfried Line. . . . 'A sudden silence falls upon the crowded room; songs of that kind are not popular with men who fight.' In this scene there comes in a newcomer to the Mess, one of the older officers who have taken on the ground jobs. He holds a very junior rank but has wings below his Pip, Squeak and Wilfred.

The narrator does not at first recognise him as *Roy*! The hero of his boyhood! The Squire's dashing and wild young son, the first flyer whom the quiet village had ever seen. He would bring his 'frail contrivance of silver, brave with Royal Flying Corps markings, dipping and circling the chimneys,' frightening the stock on the village green . . . Worshipped by the Vicarage children.

But this was 'an older, fatter Roy whose red neck bulged over his collar, whose eyes were glassy' . . . briefly, he had let himself go to seed. Badly and through the usual channel.

'I suppose I ought to call you Sir? You've been on a show today . . . Hear you lost a machine . . . I had a look at one of your machines today. They're very complicated, aren't they?' is the note of him now. 'It's a bit different, you know, from my day. There isn't—well, it's just different.'

Roy, introduced to the Wing-Commander, begins to talk, with too many 'Sirs' and reference to the '14–'18 Campaign. He is taken round and introduced to the Squadron . . . it is not a success . . . He talks too much. Laughs too loudly, too insistent in his self-deprecation—(generally a form of bragging), delighted with himself, too eager to buy a round . . . Finally he is politely elbowed out of every little clique. Roy ends up in a circle of the entertainers, for whom he has bought a round of Pimms. They at least were all listening eagerly to what he had to say.

This story is well-named *The Man Who was Dead*.

Another is called *Too Young to Live*. The mere boy who lies fatally injured in hospital talks wistfully to the comparative veteran in the next bed.

'It must be wonderful to have flown hundreds and hundreds of hours.'

'One gets used to it . . . How many have you flown?'

'Seven hours dual. Twenty-five minutes solo. It was on my second solo that . . . It happened.'

The other tries to comfort by saying he'll be all right in a few weeks. 'And you'll get the seniority anyway.'

'It's the flying I want.'

The Adventure!

The boy, as the writer describes him, belonged by rights to the Golden Age of the Royal Flying Corps when aviation was still the marvel of mankind and the country was fighting for its life, when every flight was an epic, when every pilot flew in the shadow of death, when the silly breath-taking confidence of youth came into its own . . .

Of Aviation of the Present and future? How would he have written of Cosmonauts armoured in space-suits, encased for flight in contraptions of machinery the names of which he had never heard? What would he have said of the Space-race? Of the almost casual giving out by radio that Washington announced the expectation that their 'three Astronauts would spend Christmas circling the moon'? Of the probability that 'they might come within seventy miles of the moon's surface'? Some of us are far from happy about this debunking of long cherished magic. *How sweet the moonlight sleeps* . . . ! Others are indignant because of this fighting to the death with Nature. Not even Nature as we know her, and who can be so helpful when we work *with* instead of *against* her. But an unknown hostile force, of enemy atmosphere, alien unvisaged dangers to men of our planet. How would the writer of *Night Exercise* react to those nightmares?

My guess is that he, being a Seer into the True Romance, would first experience and then could let Romance bring up the Zond Fifteen.

Lately I re-read with delight *Remembered on Waking*. It is semi-autobiographical, curiously prophetic even. A young flying-man is depicted playing chess with his father, an elderly country parson. Between two moves he breaks the news that, after the idle summer here in Wales, he has got a job.

'A flying job?' The old man (in real life I think the Rector of Arthog) is anxious when he hears that he has got an instructor's job at a flying-club in the South of England. He realises the boy has to work and must do what he likes. 'After all it's your life. Only be careful . . .'

'I'll be careful.'

But the young man becomes lost in thought, of his past, merging, growing into what was coming, tomorrow, his departure from home, sitting in the train remembering—His life in the Service . . . his pride in his first uniform and of being saluted. He would remember the bleakness of Royal Air Force stations, the exhilaration of learning to fly, the beauty of flight itself, the happy comradeship. He would remember . . .

'It's your move, my boy,' says his father gently. 'Have you been dreaming?'

His wife, who has told me of the firm unshakeable faith that the grave in Arthog Churchyard has 'nothing to do with John' and 'that he is still alive as ever he was', yet feels averse from visiting the place.

Sisters of mine, driving near, went to make sure, as John's wife wished, that the grave did not look neglected. It was in perfect order. A dark stone cross in a square of white chips, from which they pulled out the very few weeds to be found. His wife wrote back with gratitude.

I told her I always thought of him at the Service of Remembrance.

'They read out the names. You don't mind his name being read out, with the others?'

'Oh, no! *No!* I *like* that.'

I wish very much that I had her sure-set belief in survival

instead of 'a light that shifts', goes out, 'rekindling thus and thus . . .'

IV

The end of the Service of Remembrance. The singing of the hymns *O God our Help in Ages Past*, *Fryniau Caer Salem* (Hills of Zion) and *God Save the Queen*.

Then, if a bugler is available from Tonfanau Camp, he sounds *The Last Post*.

It is the only bugle-call that finishes on an up-beat note— the note of Hope.

Chapter Twenty-Five
Prince and Principality

I

'He is a very *nice* young man—'

'He is a very *intelligent* young man.'

That, at first hand and in a nut-shell, summed up Prince Charles for me by two competent male judges of men.

A woman-columnist put the same view, rather more colourfully, heading her weekly 'piece'—

OUR PRINCE WALKS THE TIGHT-ROPE WITH SUCH STYLE.

See how our Miss Anne Edwards of the *Sunday Express* hits the nail on the head!

> He faces a paradoxical situation. He is born to be King at a time when royalty has less power than ever before. Yet at a time when his own personality alone can build the Throne for a generation or bring it crashing down Prince Charles is shaping well.

She points out how he has put aside his basic shyness and reserve, how he has learnt to make friends, naturally, and to show that he likes people while at the same time he knows well that any time he put a foot wrong whether at games or public appearance, it would come under criticism, ridicule or even antagonism, and he can meet it. Certain very young Welsh

extremists threw smoke bombs at his car. He stopped, went up
to them, and asked, quietly, 'Why?'

When ignorant rudeness is countered by gentle good
manners—who's the winner?

Other times, other handicaps for a young royal.

Flash-back to 1911 and the Investiture of a former Prince of
Wales in Caernarvon Castle.

I was there.

I'm there now—So vividly it comes back!

The glare, the blare, the noise, the massed people.

Glare of a July noon. Crowds—they jam the old town—
make a London-pride speckle of faces, faces, excited faces
wherever you look. Noise, Singing, Cheers. Sun that in *splendour falls on Castle-walls*' (great play the Press made with
that quote). In uniforms and summer hats . . . Blare! Gold,
glinting trumpets from the top of a tower sound welcome to
the focus point of the whole Day! Gold on the fair head of
the slight boyish figure, almost overweighed by the ermine and
purple of the ceremonial robes in which he takes the Oath of
Allegiance to the King in words as archaic as the garb.

The eyes of Wales—an ultra observant nation!—are on
him. More unnerving, the eyes of the King who is a stickler
for every detail of Royal protocol to be carried out correctly.

Resolutely his young son goes through the drill.

'I, Edward—' and the rest of it. He, too, walks a tight rope.
But—He has, to back him, the whole force of Tradition and
the fact that he was brought up to feel that all this pomp was
the Right Thing, and that the populace, too, felt that way
about him . . .

It may be that in the strain of those long hot crowded hours
before, during, and after his Investiture he did not at the time
know (or care) that, just for his youth, looks, and charm, he
was so much *liked*?

Since that day we have fought two major wars. Lived in three
reigns. The abdication of Edward VIII. The death of well-

loved George VI. The accession of our young Queen. The birth of her four children—the eldest of whom is the Heir Apparent.

We have also experienced several revolutions. Bloodless, yes. But none the less revolutionary! Era-ending changes have been brought into the structural, social, financial life of the nation. In nothing has Change been more radical than in the upbringing and education of the Heir to the Throne.

Compare it with the boyhood and adolescence of his poor harassed and restricted Great-uncle David, whose friends were vetted, studies prescribed, every public gesture noted, approved or disapproved of by The Family. Every stitch he wore—To check up on the immense importance bestowed upon the tailoring and hair-cut of young Royalty before he ventured to set foot outside his dressing-room you have only to read the Duke of Windsor's own account of it in his book *Family Album* (of which a heading might well have been Omar's:

> Oh, many a Cup of this forbidden Wine
> Must drown the Memory of that Insolence!)

Prince Charles has escaped those shackles.

Not for him the conventional, long-vaunted Public School system, but Gordonstoun, the open air, accent on physical endurance tests, and the life required to be lived by any of the other lads. He has not been required to look upon himself and his ways as Things Apart. He has, as our popular columnist points out, been seen to emerge as just 'one of the chaps'—the all-round decent young Briton who plays cricket or polo, goes to the Ballet or the Proms, orders a 117 miles per hour M.G., wants to learn the 'cello, is interested in archaeological digs, takes pretty girls to shows, is in all these things as far from the old Establishment etiquette as Buckingham Palace is from Sydney, Australia...

... In which vast, growing-up Continent Prince Charles had spent a year of his youth before Cambridge. And, innovation upon innovation! he has to put in some time at the

University College of Wales (Coleg Prifysgol Cymru) Aberystwyth, Cardiganshire—No further away than that from
Merioneth!

II

I wrote to the Registrar of the College, Mr. T. Arfon Owen,
M.A., saying that since I lived not too far away, I would much
like to see something of the place where our Prince was to
spend some time (it would be out of term still).

It was some years since I had been in Aberystwyth. Even
then it was just to look in at my brother, to see 'Portia' (actually our solicitor) to visit friends up at the Hospital or to shop
at 'the Health place'. By the way, if we had more of these last
in every town, selling the right foods at prices less high, we
shouldn't need to build and pay for all these Hospitals.

This may be just my private, freak's-eye-view? You can't
alter it.

The Registrar wrote kindly back and gave me a date.

A perfect September afternoon! Warm, smiling, peacefully
rural. The Cardiganshire countryside through which we drove
was at its loveliest. Unchanged, the neat cottages of Glandyfi,
the small friendly wayside inn, the unspoilt vistas, the birch-
wood that would presently be 'turning'.

The road was different, though? Widened, smooth-sur-
faced, white-lined and civilised beyond recognition! Work of
those monstrous luridly yellow road-Juggernauts. We overtook
one of them lumbering to a standstill. The only hideous
utilitarian object. The only sign of Change in the Cambrian
landscape until—

We came to the top of the steep slope that leads down into
Aberystwyth town. Before the students' hostelries, before the
National Library of Wales, pride of the Principality! There,
there, joining the first breath of the sea to greet us, the Wind
of Change had blown.

We sighted the dominant tower above a long row of build-

ings. They were starkly bare, of a streamlined smooth simplicity. Clean as the half of a long pale razor-shell thrown up on
the beach by the waves of a high spring tide. Sun flashed on
glass.

Instantly, there sprang up in my mind the name: H. G.
WELLS!

For these new College buildings, up to which we drove
through a big entrance off the road, were exactly the architec-
ture of a Wells fantasy; A Shape of Things to Come. Functional. Spacious. Their lay-out in beautiful country was un-
cluttered by further ornament or elaboration. About them
were to be seen the beginnings of shrubberies, of flower-
borders and turf, but these things were kept at a seemly
distance from the windows, the long double lines of windows.
How unlike the Victorian habit of planting tall laurels right
up against their drawing-room window-panes, and screening
libraries from any view of the outer world by tall grim
monkey-puzzle trees. Here, sun and air were allies to be
sought, not distractions to be kept out.

An ideal training-place for young minds—according to
H. G. Wells' imagination.

'Imagination?' I could hear the echo of his very voice. Queer
little high-pitched squeak of a voice that still held the ring of
authority. 'Why do they all say—Look at *these*'—and I could
see him as I had seen him long ago, standing four-square by
the hall-table in his home on the South Coast. He had picked
up a sheaf of Press-cuttings from Romeike and Curtis, just
arrived by post. 'All these dam' reviewers say the same thing.
"Mr. Wells' marvellous imagination"—I *have* no imagination! None at all!'

'How can you say that, H.G.?' I asked this top-celebrity of
his day, authority of works that pioneered all the space-
fiction of today. 'Why—'

'I've no imagination,' declared H.G. Obstinacy sparkled
from his handsome features, those far-seeing blue eyes. 'My
stories aren't imagination. They're *about things when things*

P

come to their logical conclusion. That's what they are.'

He would have been pleased with the start made by this new set-up, anyhow.

'But which is the Registrar's Office,' I said to the driver. 'You should know, you brought Jean here for her interview didn't you?'

Jean, his gay and lovely blonde daughter was to begin her studies (reading Law, no less) next term.

'I didn't bring her here! This is all brand new. I'll ask one of these men.'

Workmen were still busying about.

'They don't know. I asked them in English and Welsh . . . The students aren't any of them up—'

'Ah, there's something that looks like a student—ask him.'

The profuse-haired youth in the red jersey, belted linen slacks and with a damp bathing-towel slung over his arm, told us there was nothing doing up here yet. It was—would be— the scientific and botanical side. He directed us to go right down to the old University buildings. Facing the Esplanade.

I'd known that façade. In my innocence I had concluded that it would have been demolished in favour of H.G.'s 'logical conclusion'.

No such thing.

We passed the statue of Edward, then Prince of Wales, in his robes as Chancellor of the University. A pity, I thought, that whoever the sculptor was (begging his pardon) he had made of the now Duke of Windsor a somehow less than life-size figure. Pathetically over-weighted by its Chancellor's robes . . . Since that day the news has come that Vandals have injured the statue. One deplores all Vandalism. Still . . . !

We came to the back of the promenade and its sea-views. After these buildings on the heights—Dramatic, the change from Modern to Ancient!

Cramped street, narrow pavement, an unimpressive sedate entrance beside which two amiable young ladies waited for me.

They led me through well-carpeted darkish corridors ('a step here, Miss Ruck') to a room with desks and a man with brown hair. . . . Rather young he looked to be a Registrar with all those letters after it? He was in fact not the Registrar, but his second-in-command who received me kindly and led me through more well-carpeted darkish passages past closed doors with names of their function in English and Welsh painted upon them.

I had a curious sense as of being shown to my room in some old-fashioned highly respectable, and expensive family Hotel.

Here was the Registrar's Office? Study? Reception-room? I was put to sit in a chair that would have held three of me, facing the window—I'd had a glimpse of the Registrar's tall dignified figure, and benevolent, wary, pinky face. He then sat down with his back to the window, so for the rest of the time he became a nimbus of light, grey hair and a courteous enquiring voice.

I was given a nice cup of tea and asked where I lived before I came to Merioneth and what we were doing in Caernarvonshire.

'I knew your father had been a Colonel in the Army. I didn't know he had been in the Police. For how long? Twenty years, dear me. You were at school at St. Winifred's? Llanfairfechan isn't it?'

'No: in my time it was a much more Spartan set-up, in Bangor.'

'Bangor? But it moved. That's a long time ago?'

'Yes, *very* long,' I admitted.

They were asking more questions of me politely to stave off questions I might ask. And rightly. *Security!*

I could have been sent here by one of those newsy French picture-papers who had known about 'Wallis' long before we did in Britain. I could even be the Aunt of some young man in the Free Wales Army. . . . I knew, before I set foot in that room, that all I was to be told about the Prince of Wales himself would be condensed into the two sentences at the start of this chapter.—Oh, and one other line from this scene of Hamlet without the Prince.

When I said diffidently,

'We are told'—àpropos Caernarvon being the ancient town of Segontium during 400 years of the Roman Occupation (Goodness knows what the Legionnaires, with their central heating, sunk baths, exquisitely carved ivory chessmen and the rest of the civilisation they took away with them on their recall to Rome, would have thought of some bathroom-less houses of Segontium Terrace in our time!)—'told that the Prince will be reading Archaeology here'.

'No. History.'

'Oh. Thank you.' I accepted a chocolate biscuit and gave them a piece of information in return. 'I was in Caernarvon at the last Investiture.'

They exclaimed together,

'Nineteen Eleven?'

'Yes.'

They looked at me.

The brown-haired one asked me if I was going to the next Investiture?

'*I?* Far too old now for crowds and blare and glare,' and I told them the unsuitable age I'd reached a few weeks ago.

This seemed to make them both feel somehow more indulgent to me. The Registrar said, Well, he only hoped he'd have, at *any* age, half my Vitality!

His goodbye, when shaking hands with a cordial smile, was to say (I gather àpropos the coming Investiture), 'I think you'll go.'

His A.D.C. or Second-in-command took on to 'show Miss Ruck about the place a bit'. As he conducted me into the large dim vestibule (top lights further obscured by stained glass) I realised why I'd had that sense of coming into a Hotel.

This was *exactly what it had been*!

He told me, standing by an over-life size statue at one end of it (a row of arches arched over nothing at the other end)

what had happened about the Castle Hotel of 1885. It had
cost £87,000 and had functioned for one year only. Crisis had
intervened.

'We think we have problems,' said my guide, 'but they had
them in those days too all right! They had to sell the place.
The University Committee people had been looking out for
premises. They got it for *ten thousand pounds*.'

'Good *gracious*!'

But what I meant was that if I'd had that ten thousand to
spend, none of it would have gone on *this* hideous great white
elephant.

'This is what we hope to make into the Theatre,' said my
guide; taking me on in to another large space, half-filled by a
platform, much weighty looking rubble and a group of workmen. 'We hope to put on new plays, serious drama, you know.'

'Oh, yes. That's the stage? Aren't the back-stage parts
rather cramped?'

'Well, yes. As a matter of fact, that's our difficulty. We've
had to do a lot of knocking-down. As you see. Cumbersome.
And takes such a time to shift.'

'Victorianism does.'

Wood-worn, torn-down plaster must have weighed tons.
Everything else about this tough survival of a Hotel looked as
durable as it was unlovely.

I think my guide read my reaction to Victorianism and
found it odd, seeing that I, by rights, belonged back in that
very period. In which he had not, himself, been born.

He told me the story of why a Prince of Wales (not this
one) had been sent to a certain Oxford college because it was
the only one in the University which possessed a private bathroom.

'I will introduce you to another anomaly. Our Mrs. John.'

'Any relation to Augustus?'

'Indeed no. In here.'

At a typewriter she clicked swiftly. She raised dark almond
eyes in an oriental face and smiled.

'I am a fan of yours!'

'Don't you ever wear your own beautiful national dresses?'

'No! I wear this.' She slipped off a long summer coat. A plain matching frock fitted as if poured on to her perfect slim shape. She was demonstrably vain of it—and why not?—for she was *A jewel of Asia.*

'Pleased to have met you,' she said in correct American and bent again to her typewriter. She, whose proper place was the Gem Room of some exclusive Museum of Fine Art.

'In Hong Kong she was working seven days a week,' said my guide when we'd left her. 'Sometimes till eleven o'clock at night.'

I said, as we paused outside a door marked MODERN LANGUAGES: 'Listen; I understand perfectly about "security precautions" . . . I merely HOPE that the Prince may put in some of his time—up the hill.'

'Oh, he will, he will, I daresay. *You* like that part better?'

'Much.'

'Well—' He laughed rather ruefully. 'I must confess I—I feel a certain nostalgia about the older place! The former things . . . the traditions—'

'Ah, that's having been at Oxford. I was never there.' Or anywhere else as a helpful Education for *LIFE,* until I broke right away to the dear Slade and then back. 'But I've been most interested to have seen both sides here. And thank you so much. Yes, it *has* given me something.'

Including food for thought on the way home. What would the Prince learn during these few Aberystwyth weeks of studying words of the en iaith, the Welsh language to use at his Investiture? What, especially, would he make of the Dragon that has Two Tongues, to quote Mr. Glyn Jones' witty title for a new book on Wales?

It is anybody's guess.

My own is that he will like us.

On the day that I write these words the date for his Investiture at Caernarvon Castle of the first democratic Prince of
Wales is announced for July, 1969.

The Government, we hear, is allocating a sum for decora-
tions and re-painting houses and shop-fronts along the line of
route. A face-lift for the old town?

Suddenly, I too felt almost nostalgic, as the brown-haired
man had put it, for 'the older place'; things I'd known in it,
long, long ago . . . Interval for thought . . .

III

BEFORE THE FACE-LIFT

Flash-back to the cracked slate steps, blistered peeling cocoa-
coloured paint of doors, and the general neglected tattiness of
a Caernarvon where the Castle and the Quay-walls were the
only things of beauty, during our childhood.

Yes—Fond memory casts the light around dark little caves
into which our pre-teenaged eyes so happily peered. Tolemen's
fascinating toy-shop in Pool Street! Dolls that were wax down
to the cleavage, stuffed sawdust beyond . . . And that wedge
of a place opposite the Castle moat! where you saw into a
window crammed with Welsh 'courting-spoons', dolls dressed
in Welsh costume of real red flannel cloak, striped linsey
woolsey petticoat. And a weighty wooden bread-platter with
Bara and a wreath of wheat-ears carved round its rim. Gone
. . . THE GOLDEN GOAT—How admiringly often have I gazed
up at that glittering Image, so curly-horned, so delicately
hoofed, so high-set above the Drapery Establishment!

Two larger mile-stones we knew have gone with the wind.

One is the old Guild-Hall, in which some of our Grown-ups
staged private theatricals and *tableaux vivants* (I was once On
as Little Miss Muffet) and musical entertainments were given
(in aid of the Soup Kitchen) by local amateurs. . . . Echoes

rise of that Victorian tear-jerker *Parted* (How can I live
without you? How can I let you go? I, whom you loved so
well, dear! You, whom I worship so!)

IV

Time turns the old days to derision! Ten years on my fellow-
Art-students and I would make flippant fun of the gems of
Victorian vocalists. The Bedouin's Love Song (From the
Desert I come to thee, On my Arab shod with FIRE (to
rhyme with desire)—) was the great giggle. Later, our children scoffed at our favourite musical-comedy tunes, and
presently they deserted even Noël Coward for jazz. Later still,
when I told my Sicilian grandson, àpropos the Beatles,

'I don't mind those young men but I hate their noise,'
Carlo said,

'I don't like those young men and their wigs (!) but I *like
their noise.*'

Will his descendants of the Twenty-first Century scream
with mirth over the Top-ten rave-numbers of 1980, if they
still survive to be put on the rusting old record-player kept as
a museum piece?

What will be *their* pick?

Having reached the ultimate limit of Din, listeners may
have discovered Synthetic Silence. They may switch on
appointed hours that kill all outer sound. It may be comets.
'Did you listen to last night's programme, the *Mute Symphony*
by Benjamin Husch? And oh! that glorious Third Movement
of The Pin-Drop . . .'

V

The other vanished milestone of Old Caernarvon was set
above the heights of Twthill. There it rose, it spread on a
green field like a giant white mushroom—The PAVILION.

Who remembers it in its palmy days?

How many enthralling Nineteenth Century entertainments
were set under that great round roof!

Buffalo Bill dashed on horseback flamboyantly in. The King of Quack Medicine, Sequah wrought his Miracle-cures. (Father swore he was as good as any reputable family doctor and better! Sequah could *make* people believe in his oil for rheumatism.)

Travelling Circus Variety came—Let me, for the last time, quote an obsolete lyric? 'She galloped around the arena The people all shouting Bravo! They never no never had seen a Young party such pirouettes throw!'

Nearer to modern intelligentsia-taste was the Concert of Folk-song given by singers of Wales, Highland Scotland, Brittany and Erin on the night of the Pan-Celtic Congress.

Grand Finale—the time a packed-out Pavilion resounded to its roof with the wildly enthusiastic reception of an oration given, in the vernacular, by a silver-tongued Welsh Primate . . .

Those were the days—Enough.

VI

I return you now to the 1960s.

It's a strange thing that now, *Now,* in this democratic age when, as I was told by an anti-democrat of the old school: 'The 'ole fay-çade of Royalty is what this dear Labour-Lot is out to destroy! The 'ole fay-çade!—' A strange thing that gossip about the Royal Family should be as eagerly repeated and as rife as it was in the days of Charles II.

Entries galore in the Diary of Samuel Pepys start:

Men say the King—

and report his interest in the rebuilding of the City after the Fire of London; retailing, too, his alleged *'Kissing for half-an-hour'* the Lady who sat as model for the shapely image of Britannia ruling the waves, which embellished for so long the coin of the realm.

Today *Men say the Queen*:

long ago asked for as little publicity as possible to shed its fierce light on her son. And still Rumour wags a thousand tongues. Some in wishful thinking. Some half-truths. Some founded on fact. Some, purest fiction.

Men say the Prince :

for his Investiture in Caernarvon Castle will appear in the centuries-old, traditional garb of ermine and purple, golden circlet, sword, satin doublet and hose, great-collared sweeping cloak—the lot.

Men say the Prince :

used as he's been to the casual comfort of the collarless shirt and the shorts of his long sojourn in Australia will not stand for being dolled-up in what must seem to him the obsolete finery of Wardour Street fancy costume.

Men say

that the vintage-robes worn in 1911 by his great-uncle David have been brought out of store in which they have been kept for all these years. They have been cut and altered by experts to fit this younger figure in History. Of course these are what the Prince wears on this occasion.

Men say

The Prince will be Trad.

Men say

The Prince will be Mod.

Men say the Prince

has requested that correct morning-dress of these late 'Sixties shall be the formal uniform in which he will take the oath that begins : 'I, Charles—'

Men say the Princess Elizabeth

(as our Queen then was) had replied with girlish dignity to an intrusive reporter who had asked her if it was true that she was engaged to be married to Prince Philip,

'You will have to wait and see.'

Which holds good now for all of us, her subjects.

As our columnist Miss Anne Edwards said—Immaculate topper and tails, or all-fitting borrowed flannels for an impromptu cricket-match are alike worn by Prince Charles with style. That is, he puts them on and then forgets about them. They are the right thing.

What he wears is not going to be what will count with a warm-hearted nation. Quick to note his lack of 'frills', his gentle friendliness, his yen for music (inheritance of Tudor blood) one hopes they will sing for him as they sang for his Kin.

Anyhow it's odds on that *There'll always be a welcome* will be the song in their hearts, coupled with *Hen Wlad fy Nghadau* and GOD BLESS THE PRINCE OF WALES !

Postscript

Well, I was right.

Upon the Prince's arrival for his course at the University of Aberystwyth there had been a certain sense of crisis. Tension. There had been on the one hand murmurs of anxiety ('. . . thankful when the Investiture is over. . .') on the other hand mutters of hostility.

The tricky crisis came. Not at Caernarvon's carefully, security-guarded Investiture, but at the Aberystwyth Eisteddfod of Welsh Youth which he was to open. The question was how would the current generation, the young people of Wales re-act?

The answer was to be given in two words.

In the Eisteddfod Hall, full to capacity, 'extremists' had planted themselves in front and to right, to left of the stage.

There came on the boyish, simply turned-out figure of any self-possessed, decently-mannered ordinary undergraduate of these Islands, with hardly a trace—yet an utterly unobtrusive trace there was of something 'hedged' behind the modernity.

'Boo!' was called from the right. 'Boo!' from the left. He stood there, serenely. Swiftly the disturbers were ejected. Sensibly enough, having made their protest, they went quietly.

Prince Charles, also quietly, glanced from right to left, at the empty seats.

Then he turned to face the house, smiled, and said in faultless Welsh untinged with the least English accent:

'Anwyl cyfyllion—'

(Dear friends—)

After which he *had* them.

There was not a murmur, not a mutter. People went without a tremor to the Investiture at Caernarvon.

They knew that this Prince (of Tudor descent, don't forget) who had mastered the situation at Aberystwyth, had the secret of winning Welsh hearts—Claim, if you have the luck, a share in their blood, and learn at least properly to pronounce their language.

Prince Charles, with good natural manners and tact, does not put a foot wrong. He identifies himself with the land of which he bears the title—and all over that land you hear the verdict, 'He is the best asset to Wales!'